Flowers after the Funeral

Reflections on the Post-9/11 Digital Age

Richard J. Cox

The Scarecrow Press, Inc.
Lanham, Maryland, and Oxford
2003

SCARECROW PRESS, INC.

Published in the United States of America
by Scarecrow Press, Inc.
A wholly owned subsidiary of
The Rowman & Littlefield Publishing Group, Inc.
4501 Forbes Boulevard, Suite 200, Lanham, Maryland 20706
www.scarecrowpress.com

PO Box 317
Oxford
OX2 9RU, UK

British Cataloging in Publication Information Available

Library of Congress Cataloging-in-Publication Data
Cox, Richard J.
    Flowers after the funeral : reflections on the post-9/11 digital age /
Richard J. Cox.
        p. cm.
    Includes bibliographical references.
    ISBN 0-8108-4835-X (alk. paper)
    1. Archives—Safety measures. 2. Libraries—Safety measures. 3.
Electronic records—Conservation and restoration. 4. Terrorism—
Prevention. 5. Emergency management. 6. Library planning. 7.
Archives—Study and teaching (Higher) 8. Library education. 9.
Information science—Study and teaching. I. Title.

CD971.C69 2003
025.8′2—dc21   2003007001

Printed in the United States of America

♾TM The paper used in this publication meets the minimum requirements
of American National Standard for Information Sciences—Permanence of
Paper for Printed Library Materials, ANSI/NISO Z39.48-1992.
Manufactured in the United States of America.

CONTENTS

PREFACE

This is not a book I ever intended to write, and this is not how I would recommend anyone try to write one. It happened as I worked to understand the events of September 11, 2001 (hereafter referred to as 9/11), especially as an educator of archivists, records managers, librarians, and other information professionals. A series of opportunities to wrestle with the implications of 9/11 led to three published essays and two public lectures (the latter leading to the first chapter of this book), composed and delivered over the first year after the terrorist attacks. As many of the other books on 9/11 represent, *Flowers after the Funeral* is, as I relate in my initial chapter, my effort to make sense of my own life and profession in this difficult time. Whether what follows helps anyone else remains to be seen, but the process of writing the essays did assist me in my rumination about the events of the past year.

The four essays gathered to form this book constitute four separate responses to 9/11 and continuing discussions about the events of that day. The first chapter, the most recent writing about 9/11 in this volume, was a response on the first anniversary of the terrorist attacks. The Society of American Archivists Student Chapter at my school, led by Matt Eidson, developed a panel discussion on September 20, 2002, entitled "Archives and Terrorism" and addressing the impact of the 9/11 attacks on the archives field. The panel featured Barbara Black of the Somerset County Historical Society, Dr. A. J. Plotke of AT&T/American Express, Tom Scheinfeldt of the September 11 Digital Archive, and myself. For the panel discussion I carefully outlined my comments, with no intention of writing an essay. Shortly thereafter, however, I accepted an offer to speak at the University of Maryland at College Park (the talk was given on November 14, 2002), cosponsored by the University of Maryland College of Information Studies, University of Maryland Libraries, Student Archivists at Maryland, Mid-Atlantic Regional Archives Conference Maryland Caucus, and MARAC Washington, D.C. Caucus. Being close to the nation's capital, and with an expected audience of many government archivists, I used this opportunity to flesh out my rough notes into a formal essay. I entitled it "Musing" to reflect my sense of recontemplating the events of September 11 a year later.

The second chapter, "Reacting," was originally published as "The Day the World Changed: Implications for Archival, Library, and Information Science Education," *First Monday* 6 (December 2001), and it remains available at firstmonday.org/issues/issue6_12/cox/. I have made no changes to this essay in this volume, both because it is a historic piece floating about in its early response to the 9/11 events and because it is a collaborative effort with a number of my colleagues at the University of Pittsburgh School of Information Sciences. This essay, now chapter, was made possible with the assistance of some of my colleagues, as follows: Mary K. Biagini, Toni Carbo, Tony Debons, Ellen Detlefsen, José-Marie Griffiths, Don King, David Robins, Richard Thompson, Chris Tomer, and Martin Weiss. Although I wrote the majority of the essay and provided the essay's structure, this was truly a collaborative effort and one I wish I could experience more in my own school and the field. And, of course, any criticisms of this essay (or any other of the three) should be directed at me, not any of them.

As this essay suggests, "The events of September 11 and their aftermath have numerous implications for a school of information sciences in curriculum, research, recruiting, and services to local, national, and international professional communities. . . . Information science schools can play some important, positive roles in recovering from these tragedies because they demonstrate, as effectively as anything, the unique contributions such schools can make because of their diverse expertise, interests, and programs and because of some of the unique aspects of information in this new war." There seems to have been a modest reaction to this essay within the professional library and information science disciplines (although, informally, some of us heard of its positive use in the early days after 9/11), and, equally unfortunately, our plans to build on this essay for some other cooperative projects did not materialize; I discuss some of my disappointments about the essay in the final chapter of this book. I hope that its inclusion within this volume will bring renewed attention to the essay as an early reaction to 9/11 by records and information specialists. Hopefully, continued research and teaching in schools such as mine will continue to help future information professionals prepare for such unexpected and cataclysmic events.

The third chapter represents my initial response to the events of 9/11, the need for archivists and records managers to rethink disaster or contingency planning. The essay was originally published as "Records Programs, Disaster Preparedness, and Recovery: A New Urgency," *Records and Information Management Report* 17 (January 2002): 1–14. I retitled this essay "Preparing" since it encompasses both an immediate response and the need to rethink how we plan for such horrific events in the long term. The essay plays on both the idea that information professionals had been working on disaster planning for decades, and the notion that this one terrorist attack seemed to make such efforts nearly irrelevant. While intending to provide some updated practical advice, the purpose of this essay was also designed to consider how 9/11 transformed the culture of disaster planning and response. Like the second chapter, I made only a few minor changes, leaving the essay as it originally appeared much closer to the events of 9/11. Clearly, this essay draws on the important work of so many who have labored in preservation management and business contingency planning, all of whom are amply cited in the essay.

The final chapter describes my effort to design and teach a doctoral seminar on the implications of September 11 for the information professions; the seminar title—"A New Meaning for 9/11: Libraries, Archives, and Information Technology in a Catastrophic Era"—suggests what my aims for this course were and how this course (and subsequent commentary in this brief book) fits into the themes described in *Flowers after the Funeral*. As I describe in this essay, one would expect that schools of information science, so intimately connected with a modern era often called the Information Age, would be responsive to unique and tumultuous events (such as 9/11) that are distinctly marked with information technologies. The idea for the seminar developed as I had a seminar scheduled for the spring 2002 term, one I originally planned to teach on either historical research methods or on a more particular topical area (such as the Presidential Library system, a topic reflecting my own interest). However, as I realized that the group of students who would be most likely to take this seminar was largely international students (including some from the Middle East), I opted to try to design a course focusing on 9/11 and its implications.

The idea for the essay came as part of an invitation from *The Reference Librarian*, a journal then planning for a special issue on the events of September 11. It is part of my own professional practice to write regularly self-critical essays about my teaching, both as a means of documenting what is going on in the recent development of graduate archival education and as a way of reflecting on my work as an educator. So, I might have written this essay at some point in the future anyway, but the invitation prompted me to do it in a more formal and timely fashion. My conversations with the students in the seminar—Hossam Eldin M. Abouserie, Thomas E. Dubis, Janine Golden, and Lekoko Kenosi—both during and after the seminar proved to be of immense assistance in helping me think about the course. A teacher must always have good students in order to believe that something approaching education actually occurs.

As these essays reflect, and although I am part of a school of information sciences, I have not approached the events of September 11, 2001, as a technical or scientific problem. I am not marketing myself for the many calls from government and industry to produce new techniques of surveillance and security for national or homeland defense. Rather, these essays are filled with commentary from a historical, humanistic, and, sometimes, impressionistic perspective generated from a concern that teaching information professionals requires more than knowledge about bits and bytes, algorithms and statistics, or programming and other such tools. My aim is to suggest that understanding information technology requires understanding society and its people and organizations. As we look out over the wreckage of the high-tech industry and the contradictory aims of government to protect and control us, perhaps it will be easier to comprehend such matters. The images of a burning Pentagon, a crater in a field, and a collapsing World Trade Center should aid us in recalling the limitations of our technologies and remind us of our hubris. Hopefully, these essays will help the reader to mull over such issues just a bit more.

Richard J. Cox
Pittsburgh, Pennsylvania
December 2002

CHAPTER ONE: MUSING

A RALLYING CRY?

I have no doubt that the events of September 11, 2001, will have a long-term effect on America. The horrific destruction and death came at a time when the country was mired in ruminating about its identity, vision, and purpose. Memory is mixed into history, information is confused with knowledge, and reading is associated with dissecting rather than enjoying or even understanding texts. America, already strewn with memorials, monuments, and markers, needed one with a truly national scope, and the fall of the twin towers of the World Trade Center seems to have met the need (maybe). The apparent desperate struggle on Flight 93, leading to a crater in a field in a remote area of Pennsylvania, provided heroes. And the partial destruction of a recently refurbished section of the Pentagon added a sort of symbolic message about the impending role of the military.

At any rate, at my age (I am in my early fifties), I know that the remainder of my existence will bring reminders about what happened on that day. Like the assassination of John F. Kennedy or the dramatic explosion of the space shuttle *Challenger*, we will remember where we were on 9/11 (I was playing in a charity golf tournament). If we can believe the various pundits who think either that the war on terrorism cannot be won or that, at the least, it will have no real termination, then we all realize that 9/11—with its double meaning of both marking a real date and as a shorthand for an emergency call—will be constantly recalled as a rallying point, used as part of various political agendas and personal ambitions, and pushed forward as a means of remembering what the war is about (and here the interpretations may range to encompass both a defense of democratic society and an assault on Western capitalism). The shattering collapse of the World Trade Center generates feelings nearly as deep-seated as the epic reenactment of out-manned defenders on the walls of the Alamo, the explosion of the battleship *Maine*, and the burning of Battleship Row in Pearl Harbor did in earlier eras. *Remember 9/11!*

But there is confusion in all this, too. One commentator reflects, "For many more Americans 9/11 has become a deeply personal affair. People endlessly talk about how 9/11 changed their lives, but they refer to private individual changes rather than changes within society as a whole. Some talk about how the events pulled them closer to their families and loved ones. Others find themselves permanently stressed, anxious or depressed since the events." She continues, "In fact, the more one examines the private reactions to 9/11 the clearer it is that there really could not have been one national act of remembrance on the anniversary. Unlike Pearl Harbor, when the events of one day launched the nation into a clear and focused war effort, 9/11 launched nothing comparable. The Bush administration may have launched the war on terror, but as cultural critic Susan Sontag notes in the *New York Times*, the war on terror is more like the war on poverty, drugs, or cancer. It is a metaphor rather than a real war with a beginning and end. Hardly a thing to unify a nation."[1] Many of us find this troubling.

As I write this shortly after the first anniversary of the destruction of the World Trade Center, attack on the Pentagon, and the crash of Flight 93 near Shanksville, Pennsylvania, 9/11 has already inspired numerous memorial and documentary projects, projects that in the past would not normally have occurred until years or even decades later. More than any other cataclysmic event deemed worthy of remembering, 9/11 may be the first truly Digital Age tragedy in the Western world calling on the technologies of this era, the same technologies more often characterized as threatening societal and organizational memory. Here I write with a certain amount of ambivalence and, perhaps, shame. Of course, there have been numerous other tragic events in the world, but who would have expected that the heavy global symbolism of the shimmering spires of the World Trade Center would be obliterated? The vulnerability of civilization and our way of life (which we often seem to equate) seemed more possible, certainly more so than bombing runs in Bosnia, genocide in various remote areas in Africa, and the devastation of the rain forests in South America. Our concentration of news media continuously ran the footage of the planes slamming into the World Trade Center, the billowing clouds of black smoke rising from the shattered Pentagon, and the blackened earth of a field somewhere near Pittsburgh (and not all that far from where I was playing golf). Like Oklahoma City, the reality of this tragedy was harsher because it was near home.

I felt a double embarrassment in all this. The intense focus on the attack of the United States was far out of proportion, perhaps, from the concern expressed about the brutal rapes, torture, imprisonment, and murder of political prisoners and people who just happened to be part of a particular clan, tribe, or race somewhere else in the world. Some felt it was an amazing bit of self-absorption, even with the large loss of life and the apparent surprise of it all. I also felt embarrassment as I watched the tons of paper floating about in New York City, the disruption to telecommunications and information networks, and the loss of recorded and human-held information. My own field of archival studies had been trying to deal with the threats of digital evidence for decades, and now we had glimpses of how some of the most suspect of menacing devices—computers, cell phones, and hand-held portable computers—seemed to capture the essence of the significance of what was happening on 9/11. As I became absorbed by the more technical aspects of what was happening in New York, a guilt about such speculation formed, even as I realized that it was perhaps the most normal of reactions in the face of immense human tragedy rehearsed repeatedly by the news media.

MARKING THE EVENT

The intensity of our self-scrutiny and soul-searching about the meaning of the events of September 11 appears somewhat bizarre when we realize that only a single year has passed. Over a hundred books have been published about 9/11, and here is another one. This publishing is more than self-reflection. Michiko Kakutani wonders, "The books illuminate how our self-absorbed, therapy-minded and information-overloaded society tries to process a national tragedy. They remind us that journalists are often spurred to do their best work in the shadow of others' misfortunes. And they point up our culture's penchant for merchandising every aspect of our lives, including, maybe even emphasizing what we hold sacred." Kakutani also speculates that all this writing is about "ordering, sense-making mechanics of narrative," creating story lines, bringing closure, and emphasizing the positive.[2] The "Notable Books" listings in the *New York Times Book Review* listed nine books about the events and impact of 9/11 in its nonfiction section, reflecting the immense energies involved in this sense-making exercise.[3] While I am not sure about the

positive aspect of much of the writing, I certainly concur that my
writing these four chapters is about bringing meaning to my own
self and my chosen profession in the midst of the chaos of terrorist
threats, political and economic instability, and general warmonger-
ing from all quarters. The difference here, perhaps, is that I am writing from the perspective of one engaged in managing documents of
evidence and information as material both for preserving the past
and for ensuring accountability, functions thrown into a new kind of
stark relief by the dramatic terrorist attacks a year ago.

Many of these books seem intent on using imagery, both with text
and literal images, to replay continuously certain aspects of that horrible late summer day. Another commentator about the 9/11 publishing industry also wonders "about the great drifts of Sept. 11 books
now blowing into stores and libraries," likening them to "flowers after a funeral" (suggesting the title for this book). But here is where it
all connected with me. Walter Kirn notes, "One ghostly side effect of
the Towers' collapse was all the paper that fell across the city. Memos,
invoices, Post-it Notes and letters floated on the winds as far as Brooklyn, where they settled, some still intact and perfectly readable, on
cars and stoops and sidewalks. That these documents should survive,
but not their makers, seemed almost too painful to bear, yet people
kept these scraps—stuck them in albums, slid them into drawers—
because there wasn't much else to hang on to." From here it was not
too difficult to begin to discern all the efforts to *document* 9/11 and
through that documentation to give it and us meaning. But in the
meaning and memory-inducing projects came confusion about
archives, museums, and libraries—all keepers of societal memory but
not necessarily in the manner of post-9/11 activities.[4]

The notion of funeral flowers and the proliferation of documents
was not isolated to one or two commentators. A writer for an alternative news e-journal speculates, "Laying flowers at the scene of a
fatal incident, complete with heartfelt messages of condolence and
soft toys, is now considered entirely normal. Whereas funerals are
private affairs for family and friends, anyone can leave flowers or
notes by the roadside/school gate/family home, allowing Every-
man to share in the grieving experience." However, this commentator is not altogether positive about what has been happening in our
nation since the dramatic events of 9/11: "Something is wrong with
life when every death is seen as a tragedy, and every tragedy an in-
justice. Our inability to make these important distinctions signals a

failure to understand our own human nature. This is not a call to abolish grief. Individuals should be left alone to grieve—it is the rest of society that needs to snap out of it."[5] A calligrapher and author of self-help books on social correspondence writes about 9/11 and its reflection on documentation in this interesting fashion: "At a time when our country mourned our great losses and looked to gather strength for the days ahead, we saw many images of handwritten notes—thank yous to rescue workers, goodbyes to loved ones and pleas for hope and courage. The power of these heartfelt expressions, written by hand, is clear. They serve as evidence of our collective humanity and offer some solace to our wounded souls."[6]

Grieving and solace are important, but are they appropriate representations of what archives, libraries, or museums are intended to be? In none of my comments here do I wish to be interpreted as being critical of the many projects that emerged or are being considered for documenting some aspect of the September 11 events. Much of what motivated the people and institutions behind these projects were helpful sentiments and often very professional objectives. One recent announcement about such a project states, "The significance of the World Trade Center disaster is incalculable. The media has stressed its impact on the nature of war, and on the cultural climate of this country. It will also have immense and lasting effects on the social, economic, cultural and political life of New York City, the greater New York–New Jersey region, and beyond. Recognizing the long-term importance of this event and its aftermath, a collaborative group of archives, libraries, museums, and historical records programs have formed the World Trade Center Documentation Task Force in an attempt to ensure that relevant records are preserved and that the accounts, perspectives, and actions of September 11, 2001 are carefully and fully documented."[7] Such a project certainly merits support, but the many projects and their various messages generate the need for some questions and, hopefully, answers.

Many of the projects merely reflect good old-fashioned humanitarian efforts to assist people to come to grips with life-shattering happenings. Nevertheless, whatever the motivations, reactions by people and institutions in the memory and evidence business to 9/11 do contain some easily confused and seemingly contradictory concepts, at least susceptible to such confusion by many outside professional circles (where it is often easy to lose sight of the fact that there really is not clear, accurate understanding by the public of what archivists, librarians, records managers, or museum curators do). Sometimes, it seems, another casualty of terrorism could be a clear archival purpose in these documentation projects, reminding us that through history many conquerors intent on eradicating a people or culture destroyed archives, libraries, museums, and other such repositories (including even private collections).[8] A commentator on world memory, reflecting on the situation in South Africa after the demise of apartheid, gives us a glimpse into this tradition: "The purpose of the TRC [Truth and Reconciliation Commission] is to restore memory, following the systematic elimination of the nation's archival record—a destruction that took place through decades of censorship and confiscation of materials; the incarceration and assassination of thousands of activists; and the outright eradication of state records by a governing National Party in an attempt to remove incriminating evidence."[9] The speedy response by many to clamor for a national monument or an archives or a library collection seems to reflect something of a remarkable shift of attitudes about memorialization and archives that will only be sorted out, in my opinion, in the long term, perhaps a dramatic knee-jerk reaction to all those efforts to destroy archival, museum, and library collections. And the long term, the power of hindsight, is the one thing we do not have.

DIGITAL AGE CONTRADICTIONS

Perhaps a good starting point for thinking about such matters is Jonathan Franzen's description of his father dying from Alzheimer's. Franzen reveals that in dealing with this, he and his mother stopped writing letters and started talking more on the telephone, creating a gap in his own documentary record: "The will to record indelibly, to set down stories in permanent words, seems to me akin to the conviction that we are larger than our biologies. I wonder if our current cultural susceptibility to the charms of naturalism—our increasing willingness to see psychology as chemical, identity as genetic, and behavior as the product of bygone exigencies of human evolution—isn't intimately related to the postmodern resurgence of the oral and the eclipse of the written: our incessant telephoning, our ephemeral e-mailing, our steadfast devotion to the flickering tube."[10] Franzen's lament is certainly not unique, as numerous observers are speculating on the implications of the emerging digital era for something as basic as societal memory, but his analysis is nicely made and, with the focus on the devastating aspects of that horrible disease on his father, his account is more moving and perhaps more meaningful than most.

This writer is addressing, of course, the challenges of the seeming contradictions of our modern world—the immense increase of information accompanied by an equally immense loss of information, all made more evident by the incessant conflicting claims about what computers and information do for or to us. Others have worried that the fascination with electronic information technology and information in general is crowding out a sense of the past.[11] The kinds of projects developing in the aftermath of 9/11 may include a little of this—as if we are trying to prove that all this information can be harnessed for good use in a bad situation. Yet, the self-reflection and time associated with accumulating and selecting evidence of the past is bypassed in an effort to save everything associated with the 9/11 events (even as government everywhere shuts down its portals containing information citizens should have).

The evidence that our lives have gotten more complicated can be found in many of the contradictions in our post-9/11 world. There is, for example, the resurgence of the popular notion of archives and memorials for an event about which we do not know its long-term significance. Are we interested in memorializing those who lost their lives on that day, or are we merely witnessing a mixing of grief and sentiment with a national thirst for heritage? David Lowenthal reminds us that the obsession with heritage is a kind of religious faith and art: "At its best, heritage fabrication is both creative art and act of faith. By means of it we tell ourselves who we are, where we came from, and to what we belong."[12] We need to remember that much of what now passes for heritage can be as much hucksterism and business, and we can certainly discern a bit of this in the great number of efforts to memorialize 9/11, with commemorative plates, coffee-table books, calendars, prints suitable for framing, and even websites. Within a very short time of the destruction of the World Trade Center, a 2002 calendar was available. Much of this will become collectors' kitsch in the future or yard-sale junk, except for the digital materials that will be captured in Brewster Kahle's Wayback Machine for the World Wide Web (or lost forever in the ever vacillating edges of cyberspace).

There is something slightly out of kilter with all this, especially when the urge to commemorate comes face to face with the need to document. Heritage is almost universally positive, the world through rose-tinted glasses, while records swept up as part of a documentary effort can and should reveal warts and all. Records—the kinds created in normal everyday living, business, and government as part of transactions—are not merely artifices for memory and commemoration but they are more about evidence, accountability, and other functions which can make us, later, quite uncomfortable. With the projects springing up quickly after the 9/11 attacks, one can see this tension without too much difficulty. At a panel discussion about some of these projects, an individual involved with the September 11 Digital Archive headquartered at George Mason University described the problems they had in deciding to save everything coming to them, no matter what viewpoint was evident.[13] This person also described the tension in those who viewed such a project as a patriotic effort, and who, naturally, were appalled to find what they perceived to be anti-American sentiments. But this is the nature of records and the evidence they contain; it can express or support many viewpoints, and the value of records often rests squarely on such information.[14] It will be, and always should be, the task of journalists, scholars, and citizens alike to have the privilege of wrestling with the diverse evidence offered in such records, making up their own minds about what this evidence means. If records are sanitized, culled, excised, or in any way manipulated then they lose their value and power, and a democratic society is weakened.

The immense amount of digital information generated in such a dramatic event as represented by 9/11 in the midst of a world largely shaped by the World Wide Web and dependent on telecommunications is something quite new and extraordinary. The destruction of the World Trade Center and the assault on Flight 93 revealed us now to be capturing what used to be disdained as ephemeral—particularly e-mail and cell phones (a virtual reinventing of their usefulness)—communications systems often especially lamented by archivists—as they may dilute the nature of records in favor of information rather than evidence. Before 9/11 the cell phone was more widely disdained as an intrusion on private space (forget that we all were using them), but it has achieved a kind of heroic reputation for its ability to give us a glimpse inside of events we could have only guessed about before. Indeed, our sense and hope that the passengers of Flight 93 were trying to stave off terrorists using the airplane rests primarily on the cell-phone calls coming from the plane; without them, it is likely we would never have known what was happening on board that ill-fated plane. Yet, this technology has produced some interesting and perplexing problems. Two historians studying how death is viewed in material culture capture the dilemma: "The archive-memory is one that relies upon the recording and amassing of documentation to preserve the past. . . . A further consequence of the archive-memory (especially in contemporary societies where the present is unstable and the future seems radically unpredictable) is the impulse to collect and retain everything as a potential remainder of the past."[15] While the newer technologies threaten the maintenance of information and evidence, they also create more of it.

Electronic mail, on the other hand and to continue the theme, is more often seen as a management problem, even as it is widely used as a basic communications tool. It, along with so many other computer-based communications systems, has been seen to defy the solution of its management and preservation in any practical way, even though many approaches have been suggested. Despite a generation of discussion about how to solve the challenges of digital preservation, mostly we now have an array of *potential* solutions, including migration, emulation, encapsulation, and the universal virtual computer.[16] But now we are seeking to save all those e-mail messages coming *from* inside of the World Trade Center in its last moments, even though many of our government and corporate organizations have no means in place to manage e-mail or most records as part of its record-keeping or information systems. Capturing such messages may be causing a fundamental shift in the way we imagine archives. Again, our material-culture experts note, "collective memories of past generations were further shaped by the foundations of centralized archives, museums and libraries that were open to the public." The efforts to collect all the digital stuff associated with September 11 may be part of this tradition, except that the "repositories" seem less centralized on websites. Our historians wonder, "as the media culturally available for storage have changed, from the chest to the computer, so we have seen a comparable metaphoric adjustment in the way memory is imagined."[17]

In some ways, the tragic destruction of the World Trade Center seems to suggest that digital systems are superior to paper systems, reversing the trend of what we have witnessed and debated since the advent of the personal computer. Clearly, the organizations reliant on paper records lost most of their corporate memory, whereas the companies and government agencies with backed-up digital systems were in better shape except for needing to overcome an immense knowledge-management challenge as some lost so many key personnel. All of that paper exploding out of the World Trade Center provided a new and illuminating view of the modern office. What once seemed so ephemeral became permanent, and the permanent was destroyed before our very eyes.

BIGGER FISSURES REVEALED

This failure has only a modest amount to do with technical matters, and much more to do with corporate will and desire, as well as human nature and greed. The events of September 11 brought with them a considerable amount of economic instability, especially reflected by the closing of the New York Stock Exchange immediately afterward. But the wild fluctuations of that marketplace were more the result of other factors typifying the nature of American business practice. The subsequent collapse of Enron and the revelations about Arthur Andersen's role in this, transforming the latter company, in a matter of days, from a symbol of excellence and integrity to one representing business run amok, brought a somewhat new meaning to those 9/11 images of destroyed corporate headquarters and scattered paper documents. One of the first books to appear about the Enron scandal, written for the consumer or potential stock investor and stressing the challenges of trying to determine the truth of claims made about a company's performance and potential, reveals the problem with annual reports, marred by "exaggeration and marketing hype" and making this kind of record almost a "useless artifact." The auditing process is criticized, and the authors recommend wholesale changes such as accurate communication, full disclosure, stronger accounting and reporting processes, "straightforward accounting rules," and "real accountability by executives."[18]

What the Enron/Arthur Andersen collapse represented was part of the deep cracks within American business practice and structure, problems perhaps far more complex and worrisome than the destruction of one of the architectural symbols of capitalism and the global economy (at least for the long term). What will take longer to rebuild—the twin towers or credibility in modern American businesses? I remember two separate conversations with friends who work in the investment industry, suggesting that the public revelations about these companies' practices had long been known within the business world. We were now in the realm of business ethics and basic matters of morality, but we were also scratching about in the infrastructure of business practice and expectations. One business school professor thought that the problems reflected by Enron/ Arthur Andersen were the result of "more complicated rules and regulations" than ethical matters. Robert Prentice urges business schools, and the public, to realize that business students need more grounding in business law than in ethics: "With the help of well-intentioned donors, several business schools have established business ethics centers. Unfortunately, research shows that it is very difficult to teach ethical values to undergraduates, harder still to teach them to M.B.A. students and all but impossible to get through to those enrolled in executive M.B.A. courses. If they don't get a sense of right and wrong from their families or their faith, it's unlikely a business school professor can instill one."[19]

This certainly sounds plausible, but it seems to me to go much deeper than simply a matter of making people aware of laws and regulations (although such awareness is certainly critical). By examining all those fast-selling and heavily marketed tomes on new business or management approaches, with glitzy titles promising *the* solution to how to get the competitive edge or how to operate more efficiently, we can realize that there are problems deep within the business world pushing people to ignore such rules and regulations and to view them as obstacles to success and even common sense. One such volume by one of the best-selling authors of these books reveals that policy and procedures manuals need to be sidestepped because they are "collections of 'don'ts.' And 'don'ts' stop initiative, squelch innovation, stymie creativity."[20] Tom Peters is certainly not suggesting that companies engage in illegal activity, but there is an attitude reflected here that also does not encourage these organizations to spend much time examining codes, regulations, or best practices. Book after book exhorts business leaders to be leaders by being able to understand the rules and regulations but in a creative fashion: "When quiet leaders find themselves in complex ethical dilemmas, they follow two guidelines. One tells them to take the rules very seriously. . . . The other tells them to look, creatively and imaginatively, for ways to follow the spirit of the rules while, at the same time, bending them."[21] Other authors connect these rules and regulations to bureaucracy and argue that this bureaucracy often becomes an "enforcer of corporate orthodoxies" and liken it to "molasses" that business leaders and managers have to "walk through to get anywhere."[22] Creativity, innovation, risk taking, and rule bending are all recited over and over in these best-selling business books. Technology also becomes a means to an end, as these authors argue about a new ideology of working within an organization that is exciting, compelling, and successful. One volume contends that it is not just about making money, but that working in a business is also about belonging to a company that is "equally guided by a core ideology—core values and sense of purpose beyond just making money."[23] And, of course, it is not surprising that Enron pops up in these books as a sterling example of the innovative and imaginative company: "As much as any company in the world, Enron has institutionalized a capacity for perpetual innovation."[24] The slithering away from rules and procedures is not, however, restricted to the corporate world. Government, at all levels, seems intent to do this in the name of increased security, surveillance, and protection.

The emergence of interest in documenting every aspect of an event we all watched on television and a smaller number witnessed in person is clearly the by-product of the vast information-churning and -storing devices of our digital era, but it has to be played against the complex challenges of a world that sought to restrict or avoid the creation of documentation so as to avoid compliance, skip around litigation threats, and to ensure the inflating of market value. One commentator on the movement to sweep up nearly everything reflects, "Perhaps, in our secular age, we consecrate ordinary objects to help us navigate difficult times. Perhaps, too, surrounded by a 'virtual' world, we gravitate toward the authentic."[25] But what is authentic? Somehow, we feel we were witnesses to the 9/11 events no matter where we were, and we have this feeling we cannot *not* collect stuff about it, as if it would be unfeeling or unpatriotic to do so. We have seen this before, as has been documented about the JFK assassination forty years ago, but with that event we can also see the problems it has caused. This too was a time of commemorative plates, tee shirts, and other collectibles, although we were spared for a long time the replaying of the film footage of the assassination and the funeral. We are repeating this with 9/11, except we have a vast media system in place to support it as never before; Mark Slouka, struggling with the long-term potential meaning of that late summer day, writes, "Less than forty-eight hours after the attack, commemorative T-shirts and postcards were already for sale on the corner of Spring Street. From WTC chocolate bars to personal alarm systems ('Because, in trying times like these, one can't be too careful') to Estee Lauder's 'America the Beautiful' compacts (with Austrian crystals for stars), the marketplace did its work; blurring the edges, dulling the pain, melding everything into the familiar lingo of dollars and cents. We felt better. History was once again back on the reservation. America was open for business."[26] With the JFK assassination, over time the societal archive became the media personalities, many of whom were only tangentially connected to the events of that other horrible day of November 22. The textual or documentary authority shifted from records emanating from the events and the nature of evidence blurred into controversial, conspiratorial Hollywood retellings of the assassination, mostly typified by Oliver Stone's *JFK*, which ironically led to a refocus on the opening of the records of the Warren Commission (but not until thirty years later and still not convincing to many who held to wild speculations in the void of real, substantial documentation).[27] Are we in danger of doing this again?

Embedded in this is a problem. While records and documents are gathered, the authority for their assemblage may weaken already established archives and other repositories. Ultimately, the value of what is being gathered is also weakened, as collective or public memory resides in places outside the archives, constantly shifts, and is susceptible to the whims and fancies of heritage and political agendas. While this may not seem to be a problem in that the nation seems alive and fresh with its interest in the past and commemoration of key events (such as 9/11), it can be if it undermines interest in acquiring transactional records that provide more direct evidence of an event and secure accountability of those involved. The post-9/11 activities involving archives, libraries, and museums worry me in that these institutions' historic mission can be jeopardized as their ability to hold society, its institutions, and leaders accountable is eroded in rhetoric and jingoistic flag waving. An archives needs to be able to hold all the records, ones that comfort us and ones that disturb us, deemed to possess continuing value. Was that accountability being blown out of the World Trade Center in that blizzard of records, many perfectly intact and most confidential with proprietary information? A library needs to have the flexibility to gather content for all types of uses, except now many seem more worried that a terrorist might use a library's resources to plot horrific acts. And a museum needs to be able not merely to entertain but to educate people about a society's past, not merely to become a mouthpiece for patriotism or to be confused as a shrine or memorial. In recent years we have already had some testy debates about interpreting events that ended a half century ago (such as the dropping of the atomic bombs on Japan in 1945), leaving one to wonder just how we can accurately or dispassionately build museums or mount exhibits about 9/11.[28] And the reasons for this happening now, with 9/11, seem prevalent. In looking at the *Enola Gay* controversy, Timothy Luke notes, "Factuality and fictiveness can become the objects of pitched rhetorical battles as history gets remade by museum displays, particularly if, as was the case with *Enola Gay*, many of the original 'history makers' are still around to help refine and/or define what is fact and what is fiction."[29]

GOVERNMENT IRONIES

The kinds of discourse occurring about the documenting of 9/11 as a milestone event in American history are countermanded in the post-9/11 government actions to restrict access to government and other information, best reflected by speedy and knee-jerk passage of the USA Patriot Act. Nancy Chang and her colleagues at the Center for Constitutional Rights provide a useful background to current debates with numerous references to records concerns. Chang and her colleagues demonstrate how we seem to be moving toward a government by executive fiat, including the increased examining of previously protected records or the restricting of previously open records (such as with Bush's Executive Order concerning presidential records). As Chang explains, "Since September 11, more than a thousand antiterrorism measures have been proposed in state and local jurisdictions across the nation, and already a number have become law. These measures threaten to criminalize speech and protest activities, limit the availability of public records, expand government surveillance powers, and promote participation in acts the legislature deems patriotic."[30] This suggests that the war on terrorism might already be over and lost, if we are to watch a continuous constriction of access to government information.

Such problems have become a bit surreal, as typified in the cases of former Mayor Giuliani's papers and the Executive Order 13233, signed on November 1, 2001, less than two months after the terrorist attacks, and they reveal that there are more deep-seated problems being reflected here. In fact, these two developments weave together, as strange as it may seem. I have followed the case of former mayor Rudolph Giuliani's archives with considerable interest, not because the efforts by him and his allies to move the records of his two terms in office to a private think tank are so extraordinary (they are not) but because the rationale for doing this is reminiscent of the explanation leading to one of the grandest and most expensive archival projects in history, the Presidential Library system.[31] In this sixty-year-old system we see the potential outcomes of Mayor Giuliani's actions, and they should give us pause to reflect on what is going on and what might be the long-term results. They also suggest that we might be considerably less interested in gathering up artifacts left behind at various 9/11 sites than we are in securing access to the records created as part of normal governmental functions.

What we know about the arrangement to care for Mayor Giuliani's papers is reasonably straightforward.[32] The records from his two terms have been moved to a storage facility in Queens, and they will become part of the Rudolph W. Giuliani Center for Urban Affairs, partly a policy center and partly a repository. It is obvious that this agreement occurred largely as part of Mayor Giuliani's newfound fame after the events of September 11 (his mayoral administration before then seemed to be ending in a whimper and his own credibility was strained). One of the more interesting issues at play in the controversy is that New York City has an established municipal archives, the repository for the public papers of the mayors prior to Mr. Giuliani's service. Saul Cohen, Giuliani Center president and Giuliani friend, in a letter to the *New York Times* argues that they have obtained the services of a private archival consulting firm, the Winthrop Group (which is a fine operation), because of the delays in timely processing of the mayoral records and other issues of professional standards. Mr. Cohen reports that these private archivists reported to him that the municipal archives had an "inability to meet accepted archival processing standards" and that his contract specifies that "professional archivists" are to be used "who must follow

standard archival principles."[33] The obvious point not mentioned, of
course, is that Mayor Giuliani had eight years to rectify these problems in the municipal archives, but for whatever reason chose not to
do anything. And all the various reasons for doing this, however
positive they might seem in terms of preserving his mayoral records,
still meld into the dangerous precedent of a political administration
not supporting established archives and then seeking other means
to care for its archival legacy.

All of this is eerily reminiscent of the origins of the Presidential Library system operating under the National Archives and Records
Administration. It was FDR who sought and received Congressional
approval for the establishment of the first Presidential Library. Roo-
sevelt's motivations stemmed from his concerns about the pace by
which the National Archives staff was preparing records for use, the
growing volume of records and the new technologies (especially
sound recordings) creating these documents, and the unique importance of his particular era. Sound familiar?

FDR's legacy has been the system of presidential libraries that
function as both archival repositories and museums, and some of
which have public policy think tanks associated with them. These libraries are expensive, and their success has been mixed, bringing
with them both a kind of pyramidal self-aggrandizement of the
presidents and some excellent benefits in improving access to the
presidential records. But the notion of creating a mammoth edifice
for *each* president seems excessive. And, of more concern, we have
had to endure sixty years of political tussles about the ownership of
and access to these records.

Through the years there have been countless debates and legislative adjustments in the governance of the presidential records. The
Presidential Recordings and Materials Preservation Act of 1974, following on the heels of Nixon's resignation and his efforts to control
his papers, affirmed government ownership over presidential
records for the first time. The Presidential Records Act of 1978 defined these records—separating presidential records into categories
of documentary material, presidential records, and personal
records—and made presidential papers public records under the
control of the archivist of the United States. The Presidential Libraries Act of 1986 was the result of a protracted debate to limit government support for the libraries, setting reporting requirements, architectural and design conditions, and fiscal limitations including

the requirement for an operating endowment for the establishment of each new library. And then there is Executive Order 13233, signed on November 1, 2001, with new procedures for opening presidential records involving the archivist, the former president, and the incumbent president, leading to countless newspaper editorials lamenting government secrecy and antidemocratic tendencies.

Whether or not Mayor Giuliani's records become better cared for or more accessible is not the point. He has established a legacy that pits citizens against government officials in regard to the ownership of mayoral records, and one wonders if he ever would have dared to do this had he not become a hero as a result of his leadership in dealing with the destruction of the World Trade Center at the end of his administration. Whatever the problems with New York's municipal archives or however much more quickly his papers may be made accessible, the point is that these records are public records and owned by the people. Given Mayor Giuliani's actions, no matter how well intentioned they may be, what will the *next* mayor decide to do with his records? Mayor Giuliani would be better advised to return his records to the existing municipal archives (something he apparently has done), and use his allies and resources to improve that *public* archives. Access to government information is a hallmark of a democratic society, one of the very principles Mayor Giuliani has been outspoken about since September 11. And the same is true of the efforts generated by President Bush to restrict access to the records of former presidents, both seeming to suggest that the terrorists may have succeeded, as we watch access to government records contract.

CONFUSING THE ISSUES

The irony of the ongoing efforts to create 9/11 archives and museums while access to government information is decreased as part of a reaction to terrorism, and efforts to protect the nation from it, should be obvious to most. Perhaps less understood are the misconceptions of archives and the more pervasive values of records that are being perpetuated by the various 9/11 projects. In these misunderstandings are caveats both for the professionals who work as archivists and records professionals, as well as for the public with its vested interest in the administration of records and the preservation of archives. Still, it may be difficult for many to grasp the significance of these concerns since the popular perception of archives is murky at best, modern records administration is more often equated with bureaucratic impediments to government and organization efficiency, and museums are often seen more as places for entertainment and recreation or, more recently, confused with the kinds of activities depicted on the popular *Antiques Roadshow*.

A recent book on museums captures the dilemma here, and it also has some insights into why archivists, museum curators, and historical agency folks may be responding to the 9/11 events as they are. Keith Thomson, Director of the Oxford University Museum, describes museums as both "magical places" and "dull, dusty places—institutional attics,"[34] but he wonders why, if society loves museums for their wonderful collections, are museums always in financial trouble? Thomson notes that museums "occupy a curious and ambivalent intellectual territory. On the one hand they seem to give access to the materials of our cultures, on the other they create a distance between the public and the objects."[35] Thomson also notes the challenge museums have with relating to the public since the "overwhelming majority of objects in a large museum are rarely if ever seen by the public."[36]

But it is how this museum director describes the problem with museums hoarding their collections that perhaps suggests why both museum curators and archivists are rushing to be engaged in highly public projects, especially employing the World Wide Web, about the terrorist attacks of September 11. This point is driven home when Thomson uses the popular image of archives to suggest storage and nonuse. He suggests that as museums and their collections grow, their function mutates "from action to archive." Thomson sees museums becoming archives because they begin to "acquire objects . . . *without ever intending to display them to the public*, but rather to have and hold an archive—implicitly or explicitly for scholarly research, or simply to preserve for the future."[37] With the 9/11 projects documents and artifacts are simultaneously public and preserved for future research, although the memorial aspect of these projects contributes a flavor to their work that is a departure for what most archives and museums have been involved in.

The Flight 93 Memorial Collection being assembled at the Historical and Genealogical Society of Somerset County near the crash site also seeks to save nearly everything left at the site.[38] The only exception to saving everything are living things, such as flowers (the literal funeral bouquets rather than the symbolic one of books published about 9/11). The curator and her volunteers visit the site regularly and remove what has been left, and with four to six thousand people coming there weekly (at its peak), the result is a considerable quantity of materials. The society also accepts items mailed to Shanksville and is collecting published materials related to 9/11. Everything is photographed in situ, removed to the society where minimal conservation is provided, and accessioned and stored. A year after the crash, about five thousand items had been accumulated. This collection is interesting; while the September 11 Digital Archive is building a research collection with some ambivalence about how much of it will ultimately be saved, the Flight 93 Memorial Collection is wrapped up in efforts to have a national memorial for the 9/11 victims erected in Shanksville. One senses that there are other motivations at play in this sleepy hamlet in southwestern Pennsylvania. At one discussion of this project, the curator indicated that "inappropriate" materials were not being saved, and one could surmise that these were deemed to be unpatriotic. Historian John Bodnar reminds us that the "nature of patriotism in the United States is controversial," by casting patriotism within an equalitarian society, with all the expected tensions.[39] The intense debates about patriotism and modern museums, libraries, and archives seem likely to continue playing out in the 9/11 work and perhaps in the most expressive of ways.

The September 11 Digital Archive, headquartered at George Mason University and part of a cooperative effort with the City University of New York and the Smithsonian Museum of National History, armed with funding from the Alfred P. Sloan Foundation, strives to collect and preserve all born-digital materials concerning the September 11 events. The architects of this effort decided at the outset that they would take anything offered, whatever its perspective, and the website has about 35,000 digital objects and expects that total to reach 60,000. At the site you can find images, electronic-mail messages, voice-mail messages, and first-hand narratives written after the fact by witnesses. In an interesting way, the site reveals one of the tensions evident with the 9/11 archival and museum projects, receiving a lot of criticism from individuals who expect it to be a patriotic source. Archives, while they might reflect grander world schemes to dominate society by business, political, diplomatic, and cultural means simply because of the tremendous documentation involved, are not intended to be patriotic shrines.[40]

The creators of the project contend that their objective to save everything enables them to do something historians have long desired: "The creation of the Sept. 11 digital archive and other similar projects is an indication of how the widespread adoption of e-mail and the Internet is transforming an academic discipline hardly associated with cutting edge technology. Future historians will no longer be limited to leafing through whatever newspapers, diaries and letters that happen to survive intact. Instead, they'll have instant access to a rich digital archive of Sept. 11."[41] The cynic, and it is a role the experienced archivist (and certainly the university professor) is accustomed to playing, might wonder just how well the creators of these and other projects will be able to sustain their projects and the documents they have acquired.

Archives (or museums or libraries) are not merely memorials, and they are certainly not the kind of roadside, makeshift memorials now proliferating to mark traffic fatalities and other similar tragic events. This kind of instant memorial, with individuals leaving keepsakes, has been displayed both in more substantial, permanent monuments such as the famous, and controversial, Vietnam Veterans Memorial in Washington, D.C., and in immediate response to horrific events such as the terrorist bombing of the federal building in Oklahoma City. Scholars have analyzed the placing of medals, letters, photographs, and other objects at the Vietnam memorial with great interest. One scholar notes that the stuff left there is "compelling because it collects itself." There is something special about this because it is not the result of careful museum planning but really reflects history from the bottom up. The process is both compelling and moving: "The great majority of objects mark specific individual memories, some speak to the problems of patriotism or community, some are negotiations between the living and the dead, some work to establish a community of veterans, and some make explicit political speech."[42] While archivists have worked to document all aspects of societal and organizational life, experience, and activities, and many of these records could certainly perform the kind of role delineated here by the more spontaneous and emotional process of marking what has come to be a kind of grave site, an archives also serves other purposes such as accountability and the accumulation of evidence for both scholarship and more mundane organizational functions (such as in a government or corporate archives).

Some of this kind of accumulation appears to be common to most of modern life. Colette Brooks, in her meditation on urban life, writes, "At any given moment, much of the city is lost or missing, or so it seems from the signs that appear as its citizens appeal for attention. This is how the city speaks to itself—strangers post homemade fliers on telephone poles. Bulletin boards, sides of buildings, storefronts, or the slapdash wooden fences that flank construction sites."[43] What we saw at or near Ground Zero in New York City might only be an extension of what we have been seeing in urban life for a long time.[44] Mimicking this in an archives or a museum exhibit also can be an extension of this, or, at the least, presents itself as a comfortable way for both interpreting and documenting these events.

There is another difference between the societal function of archives and that of the more intense, rapid memorialization now transpiring. Archives are usually accumulated after a substantial period of time has passed between the event and acquisition of records and the same is generally the case for museums and their assembling of objects and collections. All of this is being blurred somewhat by the archival and museum efforts to deal with the events of September 11. At the time of this writing, only a little more than a year has passed, and many of the documentary efforts were under way almost immediately after the towers of the World Trade Center had collapsed. But this is not enough time to understand events, so archivists and museum curators and others cannot understand the significance of what they are doing because the significance of 9/11 in the panorama of American and world history is far from understood.

REALITY BITES

Although moving now to preserve visual documents, artifacts, audio recordings, and other documentary materials seems to suggest that we will possess later what we need for thorough documentary efforts and an understanding of what happened on 9/11, there is an immense problem in the entire process. Edward Linenthal's book on the 1995 bombing of the federal building in Oklahoma City, appearing almost simultaneously with the September 11 attacks, commences with this assessment: "There are many reasons why the bombing in Oklahoma City resonated so powerfully. . . . The bombing in Oklahoma City killed 168 people, more people than any other single act of domestic terrorism in American history. Consequently, Oklahoma City could claim the dubious distinction of being 'first and worst' in the hierarchy of American terrorist attacks."[45] Although the attack also chilled Americans because it took place in America's 'heartland' and killed many children, one can sense how the nature of even a horrific event can be transformed very quickly. In half a decade the former terrorist attack looked very different in the larger panorama of meaning, although certainly the urge and need to create some sort of memorial was not affected. What was changed, however, was the nature of and reason for establishing both an archives and museum about that earlier bombing. Indeed, we know that all such events can change in meaning, but time passed is the crucial element. Kenneth Foote argues, "The key to understanding these sites [of violence] lies in the question of what counts as 'significant,' a question whose answer can be determined only retrospectively. Time must pass before the protagonists, participants, historians, and general public look back and assess the significance of events and struggle with their meaning."[46] And, we might wonder, just how much should pass before we begin gathering up every considerable object and record related to an event like that of 9/11?

We could probably find some archivist or museum curator out there, somewhere, who believes that everything should be saved. Recently, a book about library preservation by a well-known writer, Nicholson Baker, essentially posited the same position, arguing that librarians had violated the public's trust in them by discarding books and newspapers once they had been microfilmed.[47] Baker's writings reveal a substantial misunderstanding of the role of libraries as well as archives, or, at the least, a simplification of the missions and mandates of such institutions to be little more than warehouses. A flavor of the arguments offered by Baker is more dramatically offered in a somewhat convoluted "review" of Baker's book by G. Thomas Tanselle, the well-known scholar of printing and book history and a hero in Baker's *Double Fold*. Tanselle argues that in order to understand the history of printing "one needs originals, since reproductions offer a different experience." Tanselle then proceeds to contend that he and Baker are not arguing that everything needs to be saved, but at the same time he criticizes those who take responsibility for selecting what should be saved. Attacking my own writings about Baker, Tanselle attacks archivists: "Archivists, indeed, often express the view that they have a duty to society, and to the future, to weed out insignificant material. The arrogance of this position is astounding. There is no way for anyone to know just which artifacts someone else, now or in the future, will find of significance; and there have of course been innumerable instances of materials that were ignored at one time but highly prized at another for the new insights they offer."[48] No one said it would be easy, but only the most disconnected (from reality) of souls would take the stance that *everything* must be saved. The sweeping up of everything—all e-mail, recordings of cell-phone calls, videos, spontaneous postings at the sites, websites, and so forth—regarding 9/11 only makes sense if there is planned to be some careful analysis and selection at a later time (we can debate the time when this would or should occur).

The blanket collecting of everything and anything confuses the nature of archives, libraries, and museums and opens the door to some hard times ahead as we need to move to preserve some and not all of the documentary heritage. Since the most common record or artifact is ultimately transformed when it is moved from its point of creation, use, or private ownership to a public repository such as an archives, library, or museum, the enthusiastic acquiring of such items for even the best and most noble of reasons will create problems at a later point in time when efforts are undertaken to deaccession or reappraise them. We can see this at the Vietnam Veterans Memorial, revealing that there is a substantial difference between cultural memory, personal memory, and official historical discourse: "When individual possessions are left at the Vietnam Veterans Memorial in Washington, D.C., they become part of cultural memory. When they are then placed in a government archive, they acquire both aesthetic and historical meaning. However, the very nature of these objects, in particular their often cryptic quality, prevents them from fitting neatly into traditional narratives of historical discourse."[49] Archival reappraisal after time seems hard, as just one example. Although the concept resonates with power among archivists, the actual process of doing it seems not to have happened (perhaps because of other commitments, but probably mostly because of the public perception of the sanctity of stuff once placed in an archives).

We are left with many questions about documenting and commemorating the events of September 11. How many collections of artifacts from the new war on terror will we accumulate? If the war goes on, will they proliferate like the roadside instant monuments marking traffic fatalities? Will we be brave and smart enough to be able to critically evaluate these monuments, memorials, and archives in the future? When will that future get here? What if the war on terror never ends? What will be the long-term impact on archives as we see more and more dangers, posed by increasingly tighter government secrecy and security, both to the kinds of records created and their accessibility? Obviously, the professionals responsible for archives and records management will have an entirely different set of responsibilities in the future, and they will need to be more on guard about the care with which they work.

While it is a bit unrealistic to argue that on September 11, 2001, the world changed for good, it is certainly the case that the world has changed for a while, perhaps for the remainder of the lives of many who read this book. As I related to my students I recently read a remarkable essay by the Italian scholar Umberto Eco about his reflections on war, penned when the 1991 Gulf War was just beginning. He argues that no war any longer can be deemed just or logical or winnable. One reason is the existence of new communications, which he believes "neutralizes every surprise action," "continually allows the enemy to speak," and "demoralizes the citizens of the contending parties with regard to their own government." Eco continues: "Every war of the past was based on the principle that the citizens, believing it to be a just war, were anxious to destroy the enemy. Now information not only shakes the faith of the citizens, it also leaves them vulnerable when faced with the death of the enemy—no longer a distant and vague event but instead unbearable visual evidence."[50] Perhaps the quick memorialization and commemoration of events such as the destruction of the World Trade Center are merely an extension of the kind of communications- or information-saturated world Eco is discussing. Or, his comments are suggesting that we have become so numb about the information dousing we receive about everything, that it seems only logical, reasonable, and, perhaps, necessary that we gather up and try to save as much as possible about such tragedies.

Our society seems to have become fixated with monuments, and the number of scholarly and popular treatises about the nature, purpose, and reliability of monuments—from the most banal roadside marker to the greatest artistic expressions—suggests that we are also simultaneously fascinated and confused about what we are doing with them. Monuments erected in earlier eras often within a few generations appear to be embarrassing because of their texts and their representations, posing complex problems about whether they should be changed, discarded, moved into museums, or simply mothballed.[51] It is quite clear that monuments primarily serve the political and social agendas of the era in which they are created, as determined by those possessing the power and resources to dictate their decisions and perspectives.[52] And, we can track the shifting fates and uses of particular monuments over time, noting how their utility ranges across the spectrum of popular culture, political institutions, and all dimensions of life.[53] We all know that the decisions professionals like museum curators and archivists make about what to preserve and how to interpret their holdings are open to a vast array of interpretation and even criticism, but my concern here is that we have confused matters by indulging in aggressive agendas mostly responding to short-term and emotionally charged priorities. Of course, only time will tell. And time has a tendency to eradicate or to make meaningless many monuments originally erected as permanent markers.

NOTES

1. Helen Searls, "Confused Commemorations," *Spiked*, September 16, 2002, at www.spiked-online.com/printable/00000006DA3D.htm (accessed September 17, 2002).
2. Michiko Kakutani, "The Information Age Processes a Tragedy," *New York Times*, August 28, 2002, B1, B5.
3. "Notable Books," *New York Times Book Review*, December 8, 2002, 66–70, 72, 74.
4. Walter Kirn, "Notes on the Darkest Day," *New York Times Book Review,* September 8, 2002, 7–9.
5. Ciaran Guilfoyle, "Dramatising Death," *Spiked*, October 17, 2002, at www.spiked-online.com/Printable/00000006DAC2.htm (accessed October 19, 2002).
6. Margaret Shepherd, *The Art of the Handwritten Note: A Guide to Reclaiming Civilized Communication* (New York: Broadway Books, 2002), 148.
7. Posting of Robert C. Morris, National Archives Northeast Region and Kathleen D. Roe, New York State Archives, cochairs, World Trade Center Documentation Task Force, to ERECS-L@listserv.albany.edu, December 11, 2002.

8. See, for example, James M. O'Toole, "The Symbolic Significance of Archives," *American Archivist* 56 (Spring 1993): 234–255.

9. Erna Paris, *Long Shadows: Truth, Lies, and History* (New York: Bloomsbury, 2001), 243.

10. Jonathan Franzen, *How To Be Alone: Essays* (New York: Farrar, Straus, and Giroux, 2002), 33.

11. See, for example, Alexander Stille, *The Future of the Past* (New York: Farrar, Straus, and Giroux, 2002).

12. David Lowenthal, *The Heritage Crusade and the Spoils of History* (Cambridge: Cambridge University Press, 1998), xvii.

13. For this website see 911digitalarchive.org/.

14. See my own *Managing Records as Evidence and Information* (Westport, Conn.: Quorum Books, 2001).

15. Elizabeth Hallam and Jenny Hockey, *Death, Memory, and Material Culture* (New York: Oxford University Press, 2001), 33.

16. Claire Tristram, "Data Extinction," *Technology Review* 105 (October 2002): 37–42.

17. Hallam and Hockey, *Death, Memory, and Material Culture*, 16, 102.

18. A. Larry Elliott and Richard J. Schroth, *How Companies Lie: Why Enron Is Just the Tip of the Iceberg* (New York: Crown Business, 2002), 93, 140.

19. Robert Prentice, "An Ethics Lesson for Business Schools," *New York Times*, August 20, 2002, A21.

20. Tom Peters, *The Pursuit of WOW! Every Person's Guide to Topsy-Turvy Times* (New York: Random House, Vintage Books, 1994), 69.

21. Joseph L. Badaracco Jr., *Leading Quietly: An Unorthodox Guide to Doing the Right Thing* (Boston: Harvard Business School Press, 2002), 118.

22. Gary Hamel and C. K. Prahalad, *Competing for the Future* (Boston: Harvard Business School Press, 1994), 143.

23. James C. Collins and Jerry I. Porras, *Built to Last: Successful Habits of Visionary Companies* (New York: HarperBusiness, 1994), 8.

24. Gary Hamel, *Leading the Revolution* (Boston: Harvard Business School Press, 2000), 212.

25. Eric Gibson, "Window on War: A Venetian Blind Is Now an Artifact," *Wall Street Journal*, September 13, 2002.

26. Mark Slouka, "A Year Later: Notes on America's Intimations of Mortality," *Harper's Magazine* 305 (September 2002): 42.

27. See Barbie Zelizer, *Covering the Body: The Kennedy Assassination, the Media, and the Shaping of Collective Memory* (Chicago: University of Chicago Press, 1992) and Robert Brent Toplin, ed., *Oliver Stone's USA: Film, History, and Controversy* (Lawrence: University Press of Kansas, 2000).

28. The *Enola Gay* controversy is illustrative of such matters, and it has generated a considerable literature including Steven C. Dubin, *Displays of Power: Controversy in the American Museum from the "Enola Gay" to Sensation* (New

York: New York University Press, 1999); Martin Harwit, *An Exhibit Denied: Lobbying the History of "Enola Gay"* (New York: Copernicus, 1996); and Edward T. Linenthal and Tom Engelhardt, eds., *History Wars: The "Enola Gay" and Other Battles for the American Past* (New York: Metropolitan Books, 1996).

29. Timothy W. Luke, *Museum Politics: Power Plays at the Exhibition* (Minneapolis: University of Minnesota Press, 2002), 22.

30. Nancy Chang and the Center for Constitutional Rights, *Silencing Political Dissent: How Post-September 11 Anti-terrorism Measures Threaten Our Civil Liberties* (New York: Seven Stories Press, 2002), 136.

31. My views about this system can be found in my "America's Pyramids: Presidents and Their Libraries," *Government Information Quarterly* 19 (2002): 45–75.

32. For a compilation of materials about these records, refer to the Gotham Center for New York History at www.gothamcenter.org/alerts/giuliani/news/paperchase.shtml.

33. Saul Cohen, letter to the editor, *New York Times*, January 29, 2002.

34. Keith S. Thomson, *Treasures on Earth: Museums, Collections, and Paradoxes* (London: Faber and Faber, 2002), ix.

35. Thomson, *Treasures*, 20.

36. Thomson, *Treasures*, 59.

37. Thomson, *Treasures*, 60.

38. For information on this site and the related activities to create a memorial there, see the website at www.flt93memorial.org/.

39. John Bodnar, ed., *Bonds of Affection: Americans Define Their Patriotism* (Princeton, N.J.: Princeton University Press, 1996), 11.

40. See Thomas Richards, *The Imperial Archive: Knowledge and the Fantasy of Empire* (London: Verso, 1993).

41. For this and other documentation projects related to the events of 9/11 see the list and links on 911digitalarchive.org/websites/.

42. Kristin Ann Hass, *Carried to the Wall: American Memory and the Vietnam Veterans Memorial* (Berkeley: University of California Press, 1998), 22, 95.

43. Colette Brooks, *In the City: Random Acts of Awareness* (New York: W. W. Norton and Co., 2002), 11.

44. See, for example, David M. Henkin, *City Reading: Written Words and Public Spaces in Antebellum New York* (New York: Columbia University Press, 1998).

45. Edward T. Linenthal, *The Unfinished Bombing: Oklahoma City in American Memory* (New York: Oxford University Press, 2001), 2.

46. Kenneth E. Foote, *Shadowed Ground: America's Landscapes of Violence and Tragedy* (Austin: University of Texas Press, 1997), 28.

47. Nicholson Baker, *Double Fold: Libraries and the Assault on Paper* (New York: Random House, 2001). See my own *Vandals in the Stacks? A Response to Nicholson Baker's Assault on Libraries* (Westport, Conn.: Greenwood Press, 2002).

48. G. Thomas Tanselle, "The Librarians' Double-Cross," *Raritan* 21 (Spring 2002): 252, 258.

49. Marita Sturken, *Tangled Memories: The Vietnam War, the AIDS Epidemic, and the Politics of Remembering* (Berkeley: University of California Press, 1997), 3.

50. Umberto Eco, *Five Moral Pieces*, trans. Alastair McEwen (San Diego, Calif.: Harcourt, Inc., 2001), 9.

51. Sanford Levinson, *Written in Stone: Public Monuments in Changing Societies* (Durham, N.C.: Duke University Press, 1998).

52. Kirk Savage, *Standing Soldiers, Kneeling Slaves: Race, War, and Monument in Nineteenth-Century America* (Princeton, N.J.: Princeton University Press, 1997).

53. John Seelye, *Memory's Nation: The Place of Plymouth Rock* (Chapel Hill: University of North Carolina Press, 1998).

CHAPTER TWO: REACTING

INTRODUCTION

On September 11, 2001, the terrorist hijacking of four domestic air flights led to the destruction of the World Trade Center in New York City, an attack on the Pentagon, and the loss of thousands of lives. News reporters, commentators, various experts, and political leaders all commented, in sobering fashion, about our world changing in a matter of hours. The issue of the *Economist* (September 15–21, 2001) appearing immediately after the disasters featured a dramatic photograph of the collapse of the World Trade Center with a banner headline reading, "The Day the World Changed." It was to be an image we would see over and over again, on magazines, book covers, postcards, and nearly every surface where one could post a message of outrage. The lead article in that issue compares the attacks to the 1941 attack of Pearl Harbor, stating, "This week has changed America, and with it the world, once again."[1] It was a message we would hear again and again, as well.

We can argue about whether any such event, even one this horrific, can be given a moniker indicating such change at a point in time that is still so close to the events. Some commentators are already doing this. Stanley Hoffman focuses on the terrorist attacks as the by-products of a "global society," noting that this was particularly troublesome for the United States, the "country that has done most to destroy borders and walls, to shape a world market, to promote freedom of communications, information, and movement."[2] Likewise, Lewis H. Lapham wonders why so many commentators thought these events were "unbelievable," asking, "Do the merchants of the global economy not read their own sales promotions?" Lapham muses, "Whoever organized the attack on the United States clearly understood not only the arcana of postmodern finance capitalism but also the idiom of the American news and entertainment media."[3] Some historians have indicated already that all of the hyperbole about the "newness" of what occurred on September 11 may be part of the general tendency by the media, politicians, commentators, and others to forget about previous conflicts that the United States has been engaged in.[4] Anyone taking the longer, historical view of the uses of information sources, repositories, technologies, and systems has also resorted to similar conclusions, urging care in assessing the implications of a *present,* still *unfolding* event.[5] We would be remiss, however, if we ignored the consequences of these dramatic events on what we are about in a school of information sciences, especially since so much of the history of information science is tied up with wars, both hot and cold.[6]

Faculty, staff, and students at the University of Pittsburgh School of Information Sciences did not need to be told about the transformation of their world. Haunting images on television and the World Wide Web of paper records drifting through lower Manhattan, reports of dramatic uses of cellular telephones by victims, and descriptions of law enforcement agencies tracking alleged terrorists through the use of credit cards and other records and information systems (related to automobile rentals and activities at airlines, flight schools, and hotels) all attested to the role of and impact on modern information technologies and systems in these events. The unique role of information systems even led to some interesting efforts to memorialize the victims of the September 11 events by saving any recorded material chronicling history of the World Trade Center and the attacks that destroyed it, focusing on "sounds from dictation tapes, tourist videos made before Sept. 11, training films used by World Trade Center tenants, audio recordings of financial transactions or any other 'shards' of sound that capture the expressions, exchanges, and humanity that defined the buildings"[7] (efforts discussed in chapter 1). And, everywhere we looked we saw libraries, librarians, archivists, records managers, and other information professionals offering services, many harnessing the power of the Internet to build websites with useful information and news for individuals needing advice, help, consolation, and other information in the aftermath of the events.[8]

Early indicators were that the events of September 11 had much to do with what goes on in a school educating future archivists, librarians, information scientists, knowledge managers, and other information professionals. We learned that libraries, archives, and computer systems were destroyed or severely damaged,[9] but the impact was much more profound. The *Economist* perceptively notes that "counter-terrorism" depends on both the "pooling of information" and "international co-operation," and with this we have a glimpse of the possibilities of the first warfare in the Information Age.[10] An article in the peer-reviewed electronic journal, *First Monday*, describes the concept of "netwar": "Netwar is an emerging mode of conflict in which the protagonists—ranging from terrorist and criminal organizations on the dark side, to militant social activists on the bright side—use network forms of organization, doctrine, strategy, and technology attuned to the information age."[11] Investigative reporters concentrated on intelligence-gathering systems, an integral part of the Information Age and its origins.[12] We are a school intimately connected to whatever passes for the Information Age, even though our tendencies, those of the faculty and students, would be to debate the precise meaning of the Information Age. The meanings of an "Information Age war" or a "netwar" might be even muddier and more debatable *except* for the fact that it was being played out before our very eyes. The technologies of a "netwar" suggest that no matter how we define such terms, the prospects of future warfare have much to do with what we teach and research at a typical school focused on the various components of information science, as terrorist and other groups "take advantage of networked designs" and we observe a "new generation of social revolutionaries, radicals, and activists who are beginning to create information-age ideologies, in which identities and loyalties may shift from the nation state to the transnational level of 'global civil society.'"[13] From the mid-nineteenth century we have witnessed an increasing ability to record and report on warfare, from the early uses of photography to the later role of television,[14] but what we are now involved in may be the first war in which the media is used both to report on or document a war *and* to wage it. An article in the *Economist* reflects on precisely this link of war and technology: "During the American Civil War, journalists using the then newish technology of photography traveled with vast arrays of equipment . . . which had to be packed on to large, horse-drawn carts. Since then, many wars have been touched by improvements to the technology of reporting. In the first world war it was film; in the second, live radio; in Vietnam, television. The star of the current conflict in Afghanistan is the video satellite phone."[15]

The events of September 11 and their aftermath have numerous implications for a school of information sciences in curriculum, research, recruiting, and services to local, national, and international professional communities. Obviously, many other university faculties and professional schools also perceived the need to address the nature and impact of the September 11 events and the ensuing war on terrorism.[16] Information science schools can play some important, positive roles in recovering from these tragedies because they demonstrate, as effectively as anything, the unique contributions such schools can make because of their diverse expertise, interests, and programs and because of some of the unique aspects of information in this new war. Surprisingly, early descriptions of responses by professional schools to the September 11 events included every kind of professional school *except* information science.[17]

This essay is intended to rectify this omission. What follows is a discussion of a set of broad topics relating to the World Trade Center and Pentagon attacks and their aftermath in which a school like this already possesses expertise and can contribute in profound ways. There is no particular order to the topics, given that they are interrelated and, in most cases, of equal importance. There is also no profound conceptual framework for this discussion. We could place these concerns into some configuration of information documents, technologies, and communities (or something else like this) reflecting what we do and teach or what we theorize about and conduct research on, but this seems premature at this early date. There are also some more personal human costs to the September 11 events that are difficult to process as well. At this point we know of at least one graduate of our school who lost her life in the World Trade Center destruction. We are also witnessing some unfortunate losses in international students who are leaving to go home and some poor treatment of Islamic and Middle Eastern students. The personal dimensions of the World Trade Center destruction and the Pentagon attack themselves stimulate important issues about the uses of information, information technology, and other related matters intricately connected to a school like this.

SHIFTING PARADIGMS?

For decades, most of the world's enterprises—commercial, governmental, medical, and educational—have discussed moving their internal information from paper to electronic information and recordkeeping systems. This "paradigm shift" (however overused this phrase seems, it still appears valid[18]) was thought to be a gradual process—

accelerated by the efficiency of the new technology, but slowed by the costs of equipment, of converting archival data, and of training. On September 11, this process seemingly ceased to be gradual—the paradigm now seems to have fully shifted. It seems that firms that relied more heavily on information technology (and maintained appropriate off-site backups) will be the ones to recover most quickly from this disaster. More than ever, the watchwords of this new era will be digitization, decentralization, security, and survivability. Schools of information science must reflect this shift in their curriculum and research and acknowledge that they have roles to play in helping organizations, governments, and professionals to prepare for coping with this shift. Researchers were calling soon after the attacks for Congress to provide more funding for studies in cyberterrorism: "William A. Wulf, president of the National Academy of Engineering, said research into network security hasn't advanced much in the past two decades. 'Frankly, I was simply appalled by how very little progress had been made in the past 15 years,' Mr. Wulf said. 'Our research base in computer-network security is minuscule.' Most computer firewalls are about as effective as the Maginot Line, which France had hoped would protect it from Germany in World War II, he said."[19] Again, we seem immersed in a new kind of war with direct ramifications for a school of information sciences.

As leaders in information applications and technologies, such schools have an obligation to the information industry, its clients, and all institutions (government, business, educational, and cultural) relying on increasingly sophisticated uses of information. They must convince everyone that the paradigm has shifted, and why—recognizing that there will continue to be needs for the maintenance of some traditional information sources for historical, cultural, and other reasons.[20] Such schools can research ways to ease the rapid shift that enterprises must make, and they can educate and train the people who will lead and implement the shift. Such schools can serve as both examples and as laboratories for research, reflecting their unique nature as professional schools within universities contributing to scholarship and education while sending out practitioners such as archivists, librarians, software designers, information policy specialists, managers of information systems, and Webmasters.[21]

The events of September 11 and their aftermath provide another profound possibility for information science schools, that of explaining the nature and importance of information technologies and their uses to the public and policymakers in new ways. In the past information technologies have tended to be publicly discussed as either the route to the destruction of or salvation for society.[22] And, in most cases, the faculty of information science schools have not been involved in the public forum, at least in terms of writing widely for public debate and consideration.[23] Recent events may have changed this, opening up new possibilities for the involvement of information science schools and the opportunity for their faculty to explain what they do. Stephen Jay Gould writes that he believed that "science is wonderfully accessible, that most people show a strong interest, and that levels of general learning stand quite high . . . but that we have mistakenly failed to include the domains of maximal public learning within the scope of science." Gould, in driving home his point, then remarks that the inability to play the violin does not diminish the capacity to enjoy music, that the inability to read ancient languages does not mean we cannot read and comprehend Homer, and that a lack of mathematical understanding does not mean someone can't learn about the differences between quarks in particle physics.[24] The use of the media, cell phones, the Internet, and other information technologies in the events of September 11 all suggest that information science schools have a distinct advantage in conveying the significance of what they are about because of the pervasive use of these technologies by a wide spectrum of individuals.

A POTPOURRI OF ISSUES

Disaster Preparedness and Recovery

The images of paper records were haunting. A *New York Times* article starts its report in this way: "A crumpled page of cleaning instructions with a reminder to damp-wipe smudges and smears. A blank check from a financial firm on the 101st floor. A tattered résumé, shreds of a faxed message, a cell-phone bill, a note about school, a bank statement, an expense report. A request for a promotion dated 1979." The article continued: "Personal and official, all shapes and sizes, bits of paper blanket Lower Manhattan with the mundane poetry of office life. They drifted from the sky on Tuesday and fell to earth miles away in Brooklyn, sheets and scraps that document the 28-year life and abrupt death of the World Trade Center."[25]

While immediate concerns focused on the loss and saving of human lives, the large concentration of major financial firms and government agencies in the World Trade Center also brought concern for the recovery of records (both paper and electronic) and information systems. Experts on the recovery of such systems estimate that within five years of major disasters, two of five companies go out of business,[26] indicating that the consequences of the terrorist attacks are indeed long-term ones.

The World Trade Center destruction is perhaps the most dramatic reminder of the need for companies, governments, and other organizations to be prepared for unforeseen disruptions in their normal activities and the sudden loss of information and records systems. Indeed, the World Trade Center occupants were perhaps better situated than most to deal with cataclysmic events because it was a terrorist target in 1993.[27] One estimate suggests that this was the "largest-ever mobilization of computer backup tapes to help companies reassemble their business information," with as many as two million tapes sent to companies affected by the World Trade Center destruction.[28] Organizations need to plan in advance for the use of temporary facilities, alternative systems for communications, and risk analysis for the recovery of information and evidence. John Jackson, president of the disaster-recovery division for Comdisco, of Rosemont, Illinois, while noting that electronic systems were routinely backed up and perhaps not affected, comments in one interview that "there's a lot of paper-based information in offices." Jackson continues, "We have really not, in the 17 years I've been in the industry, had a smoke-and-rubble event of this nature. This will test recovery plans in a way they have never been tested."[29] On the other hand, there is a sense that many of the organizations and companies, especially the law firms and government agencies, located in the World Trade Center were just as dependent on the paper records that were destroyed and whose recovery had to take backseat to the rescue efforts of individuals injured and trapped in the buildings' collapse.[30]

The implications of the destruction of paper and electronic information systems are immense for a school of information science. After all, technology and disaster have long been recognized as being commingled.[31] The faculty teaching in such schools need to understand why the enterprises inside the twin towers were still tied to paper-based commerce and documentation. Faculty in the school and their students need to research better techniques that ease the transition from paper to electronic systems, and they need to address whatever reasons are given for these enterprises' resistance. The importance of data replication and reliable network design was underscored by this disaster, and information science faculty and other experts must do more research in these areas.

The faculty and experts must also seek to understand the resilience of paper documents, both identifying aspects of work where paper seems to be superior (or at least relied on, suggesting that it is the superior medium) and procedures for ensuring that there are adequate mechanisms for safely managing these documents and ensuring their recovery in times of disasters. Steve Hensen, the president of the Society of American Archivists, muses that "it is an eerie irony that virtually the only thing that has survived the mass destruction of the World Trade Center is paper—much of it singed and dusty, but intact nonetheless. The streets of lower Manhattan along with the graveyards of Trinity and Grace Churches lie several feet deep in memos, letters, resumes, accounting records, reports and other papers that were at the core of the business of early Tuesday morning and that would have eventually found their way to our repositories."[32] The implications of the disaster have far reaching consequences, obviously, for the vast array of constituencies and disciplines that an information science school works with, serves, and educates people to work in.

Whether the paper records seen drifting about Manhattan were the official records of companies and government agencies or merely convenient paper versions of electronic records is intriguing, but it might be beside the point. In educating future records, library, and other information professionals, information science schools must prepare them to assume roles in which they can advise their organizations about how to best prepare and maintain their records and other information systems in case of natural or man-made disasters. Their faculties need to consider how disaster preparedness is integrated into the curriculum so that all students are equipped to assume such a function in their institutions and how they can design and offer workshops and public presentations about the importance of disaster preparedness in order to offer their expertise as a service to help their regional companies, governments, and other institutions be prepared for disasters of any kind. We must be able to understand how disaster preparedness and recovery concepts and practices have been altered by the new threats of terrorism.[33]

Reports about efforts to recover information and records systems also described the growth in this industry in recent years.

One article noted that manufacturers of back-up and recovery software had $2.7 billion in revenues last year, and that figure is expected to grow to $4.7 billion in 2005. The World Trade Center destruction and Pentagon attack may increase this growth.[34] As a result, these faculties need to evaluate how their academic programs support students who might be interested in preparing for careers in recovery systems and disaster preparedness. There may be particular parts of the landscape of companies and organizations requiring special attention. For example, initial estimates concluded that 14,000 of New York City's 76,000 lawyers had lost or been displaced from their offices, hampering their work that was already compounded by the fact that many of the law firms did not have adequate disaster or contingency systems for recovery of lost information.[35]

Disaster preparedness, and in fact sound management, must address true knowledge management as well. Many information science schools already had established or started developing knowledge-management programs before the attacks on the World Trade Center and the Pentagon. Some might contend that although the term is new, its practice and comprehension of its importance date back many decades or even longer. In addition to helping us determine when and how to use paper and electronic information systems throughout an organization to manage the organization most effectively, the September 11 events also highlight the enormity of the loss of human life and human memory. While we continue to make great progress in developing information systems, the field of knowledge management is still in its infancy. Capturing knowledge held in people's memories and based on assimilation and integration of facts, information, life, and experiences, and determining how to incorporate this all into improving processes, procedures, and thinking within an organization are daunting challenges. Much of what was in the memories of the thousands killed on September 11 will never be recovered. What brings the notion of knowledge management together with the September 11 tragedy is that we now have technologies and systems that make the study and practice of knowledge management more feasible.

Knowledge Management

A central tenet of knowledge management (KM) is that humans are critical information resources for organizations, not only as complements for paper and electronic information sources but as unique

sources that make these systems understandable and usable. The use
of the KM term has gathered momentum in businesses and other organizations, most probably because it is convenient to use the term
as an umbrella for efforts that seek to facilitate intraorganizational effectiveness through the utilization of informal, tacit knowledge pos-
sessed by human beings employed in organizations; to facilitate
intraorganizational effectiveness by providing the ability to discover
and access knowledge in documents (*documents* are defined broadly
as any intellectual artifact produced by an organization including
data, databases, memos, technical reports, manuals, and presentations);[36] and to promote effective interorganizational and customer
relationships through such means as competitive intelligence and e-
commerce.

Knowledge management addresses concerns prevalent in organizations today. The first concern is related to productivity and return
on investment. A growing number of organizations, faced with evidence indicating that information technology alone does not increase productivity, seek to leverage their investments in information technology by focusing on the development of management
information systems that provide users with access to relevant data
and information resources, and that afford parent organizations
with a sustained return on the investment made in the generation,
procurement, and maintenance of data and information resources.[37]

The World Trade Center destruction and Pentagon attack brought
KM into stark relief. John Jackson, speaking from the perspective of
a disaster-recovery company that recovered data for companies affected by the 1993 World Trade Center attack, notes that normally
lost data could be retrieved through paper records *or* employees'
memory. Jackson states about the recent World Trade Center destruction, "in this case, all the paper is gone because the building is gone.
The employees who might otherwise have been able to re-create the
transactions might've been killed."[38] Donald Haisman, a certified financial planner in Fort Myers, when interviewed about the potential
chaos inflicted on individual investors by the attacks, was more concerned with the loss of the people than the records or systems, refer-
ring to this as "intellectual destruction."[39] At the Pentagon, a budget
office staff was nearly wiped out, and office records for the past year
had to be re-created through the use of volunteers, retired workers
coming back, and other means. The office's director stated, "You
couldn't get a fix on who was missing. In a normal process, you

would rely on a supervisor where their employees might have been. In our situation, there were no more supervisors." Another office worker stated, "We lost every single paper in the office, We lost all three of the servers that stored all our electronic information, and so when we came in, the task was basically, reconstruct a whole year's worth of activity for $3.6 billion, and you've got 10 days to do it."[40] The scale of such destruction is somewhat unprecedented, and it places a new demand on the concept of knowledge management and, as a result, a new demand on how the information science schools integrate knowledge management throughout their curriculum. The World Trade Center disaster provides a focus for how knowledge management connects with other tools and approaches such as artificial intelligence and data or document management.

With the September 11 events and the continuing discussions about the recovery efforts, most information science schools will recognize that they need to develop KM curricula and research and service programs at undergraduate, master's, and doctoral levels and in continuing-education opportunities. The importance of KM will very likely lead to a greater emphasis on it in other specializations in such schools. For example, the present stress in information science schools on archives and records management will emphasize more equipping students to be experts in records and record-keeping systems and to understand their importance for purposes of evidence, accountability, and corporate or societal memory.[41] Knowledge management is an integral part of this curriculum, implicitly and explicitly, and archives and records-management programs can be both a bridge to KM programs or be changed to accommodate a greater KM emphasis. In all such efforts, there will be efforts to educate individuals to understand how human resources connect with technology, rather than stressing technology as an end in itself. Again, the human dimension of the September 11 events make this all the more obvious.

Courses in archives and records management, telecommunications and information systems, networking, policy, ethics, library and information services, security, and many other areas need to reevaluated in schools of information science as a result of the events. Knowledge management is an area lending itself well to a set of short-term continuing-education offerings, directed at the companies, governments, and other organizations located nearby such schools. The World Trade Center destruction and recovery efforts by

companies for restarting their operations can provide numerous relevant case-study materials for such workshops, while helping these
schools to provide a real service to their regions. Such continuing-
education efforts can highlight the graduate programs at these
schools and foster partnerships with regional organizations interested in the issue of the human intelligence aspect of records and
information-systems technologies.

Workplace Design and Location

The destruction of the World Trade Center, a symbol of American
and international commerce and home of many leading financial
and other companies, led to the loss of millions of square feet of
prime Manhattan office space. The twin towers represented ten million square feet alone and early reports indicated that the loss of this
space would spike up costs for offices and lead to a scrambling by
financial, government, legal, and other organizations to find re-
placement offices to continue operation.[42] Disaster-preparedness
plans relating to electronic information systems provide for the
staffing of temporary offices, called "hot" sites, fully equipped with
computers, Internet access, and other office equipment. The question looming in the background may be whether these companies
will opt to relocate into large offices such as what the World Trade
Center represented, and, indeed, debate about this began almost immediately after the destruction of the twin towers.[43] Matters of security and worker confidence may override matters of clustering
large companies into single buildings even if the technology allows
such concentrations. However, the reconstruction of new buildings
at the World Trade Center site might provide an opportunity to
build a facility drawing on all of the most advanced information and
other technologies that address both workers' performance and
safety. A new facility, with better integration of data, information,
and knowledge systems might ensure the better protection of such
information resources.

After these events, many companies may opt for the use of video
teleconferencing as a means of restricting travel and clustering of
large groups of staff into single locations. As one report suggests, the
temporary displacement of the firms may lead to a dispersal of companies that may make it difficult for them to consider relocating in
New York City since "commercial real estate brokers have begun

looking as far away as Upstate New York for available space for some displaced companies."[44] Another report notes, "It was largely because of the multiple communications options available to them, for instance, that executives and other professionals who found themselves far from home base because of the disruption to airports last week were able to do business in 'real time' even as they rented cars or hopped on trains for slow transcontinental trips home." This experience, even under such adverse and tragic circumstances, might persuade many companies to use such technologies in a more pervasive and organized fashion in order to minimize travel or the need for concentrated physical offices. The same commentator argues, "But in pure technology terms, the World Trade Center model of commerce seems no longer necessary. And if much of 'Wall Street' ends up moving permanently to its currently temporary quarters in Jersey City, or dissipates more than ever into cyberspace, it may indicate just how much the physics and physical realities of the modern financial system have truly changed."[45] These tragic events may provide an opportunity for the predictions of virtual workplaces and even virtual cities to come to fruition, in a manner similar to what has happened in the past with urban and social planners facing other cataclysmic events.[46] Such matters reflect long ongoing debates about the centralization or decentralization of management and how supporting information systems are analyzed, designed, and implemented (again, the kinds of tasks that library and information science schools have long been concerned with).

Academic programs at schools of information sciences have long been concerned with how workplaces function, especially in the design regarding the use of information technologies and the storage and use of information. Interests range from the implications of new and emerging electronic information technologies for how organizations work and the kinds of spaces needed to the matter of how the need for organizations to use both electronic and paper documents affects the design of office space, work flow, and information storage and security. The use of video teleconferencing poses, for example, some interesting questions. While we encourage the use of video-conferencing technology, we must be compensating for the lack of direct interpersonal contacts and researching new ways to provide realism at low prices, much in the fashion that psychologists and others have cautioned us about the growing use of the Internet for human communication and interaction.[47] The September 11 events also suggested the strengths and limitations of other telecommunication systems. Damage to the New York Telephone Building, built in 1926, housing Verizon Communications demonstrated that the telephone system was vulnerable because of the concentrated location of the telephone infrastructure and the heavy reliance on dedicated data lines used by big corporations, financial institutions, the regional medical-library program for at least three states, and other organizations.[48] In these and other aspects of the use of information technologies, faculties at schools of information sciences will need to reevaluate how they teach, how students learn, the nature of their research, and the knowledge and skills they impart to their students. The experience many of these schools are gaining in web-based education also is adding to this area of inquiry.

In the aftermath of September 11, one of the many interesting stories to emerge is the role played by the NYC Wireless. NYC Wireless (www.nycwireless.net) is a community-based project designed "to take use of the airwaves for the purpose of providing distributed, free, always-on mobile Internet access through the IEEE 802.11b wireless local area networking standard" by providing a platform and medium for community-based networking and content development. Using inexpensive equipment that can be purchased off the shelf of most retail computer and electronic stores, e.g., the LinkSys Wireless Access Point, NYC Wireless provided Internet access to emergency and rescue workers in the immediate aftermath of the collapse of the World Trade Center towers, and in the days thereafter also assisted businesses and individuals who needed Internet access and had the means to employ NYC Wireless's capabilities.

What is the significance of NYC Wireless in the context of Library and Information Science (LIS) education? It may be twofold. First, it speaks to the value of open, community-based services (and while NYC Wireless does not unto itself suggest this, it serves as an example of the type of community service that should be viewed as an integral part of LIS education). Second, the fact of its existence is an indication that wireless technology is quickly going to form an important platform for information service, and yet another technology environment in which libraries in particular will be challenged to compete.

At present, library and information science schools often focus primarily on traditional information providers, such as libraries, archives, museums, and organizations of all types. They need to assess whether the present curriculum is supporting serious discussion and education for students about how present workplaces need to evolve to provide security, delivery of information and other services, and adequate environments for individuals working in the offices. The faculties of these schools bring many different perspectives on such matters, ranging from ergonomic issues to the uses of telecommunications, and this area opens up many topics for research and development projects as well as teaching and curriculum revision.

Technology and the Human Dimension: Cell Phones and Children

Traditionally, information science faculty have had varied opinions about the importance of the human dimension in information-technology systems, if not in the ultimate use and intention of these systems at least in how and what they stress in the classroom and in their research. The events of September 11 bring into focus just how information content and information technologies possess a real human face and what the various faculty and programs have to offer about understanding the human dimension. Even programs such as telecommunications, the most technically oriented of these schools' degree programs, often have courses in "human communications," and all programs include the human dimension to varying degrees.

The important role that cell phones played in the events of September 11 illustrates that wireless communications is more than a technology and reflects the importance of courses such as what has been offered in telecommunications programs and in information science schools. These and other library and information science disciplines need to offer courses describing the impacts of communication that is broadband (fiber) and mobile (wireless), teaching their students the potential applications and the social and societal impact these technologies bring. This presents opportunities for more cross-departmental and cross-university development of courses or cross-listing of courses, bringing together faculty from the many specializations represented in such schools to focus on topics of mutual interest. Studying the impact of the failure of such reliance on teletransmission and telecommunication systems is an important component in determining how such systems should be designed with backup and recovery plans.

The aftermath of the September 11 attacks brought reminders of the issues related to the use of telecommunications technologies, especially the human dimensions of the use of the technologies. On television, we saw many talking heads whose lips were not synchronized with the accompanying audio. We must learn which communication technologies the broadcasters are using and understand why some of them performed so poorly for this application. We also need to understand the economics that made the broadcasters abandon satellite feed, which didn't have this problem. We must research ways to make this new technology work or we must invent an even newer technology that can provide acceptable and economic communication of talking heads. Amidst the tragic aspects of the events, we were handed a laboratory regarding how information technology performs when pushed to its limits and this provides the information-science-school faculties both an opportunity to develop useful, practical teaching case studies and to identify topics and issues for them and their graduate students to research in the future.

The human dimensions were also evident beyond the flaws and problems of the uses of information technologies in reporting on the events of September 11. One of the most profound aspects was the concerns and issues generated about meeting the information and resources needs of young people, reflecting a long-standing area of teaching in many information science schools, especially those that have built off of the older library schools and continue to maintain programs preparing people to work in public and school libraries. The human dimensions also can serve as a vehicle for bringing disparate parts of these schools together in different ways. For example, the traditional departments of library science often have had a longtime stress on children and youth services. There was considerable discussion about the impact of the television and newspaper images on children, and this opens up the possibilities for considering across the curriculum how such matters can be introduced to the wide range of students in all specializations. Unfortunately, in many schools students with more technical rather than service orientations and vice versa tend not to mix or to work together as often as they could. The schoolchildren suggest why we need to do better in bringing the diverse students and faculty together in more creative ways.

On the morning of September 11, 2001, 5,629 students in seven elementary, middle, and secondary schools in the immediate vicinity of the World Trade Center were in class.[49] Within hours their world had changed as well. Dismissed from school, some reunited with their families, some waited for word of a parent; formal learning was abruptly interrupted. When they returned in a week, it was to different schools with different students. By the beginning of October, it was clear from observed behavior that many students were experiencing emotional upheavals.[50] Teachers and parents—also facing feelings of fear, anger, and grief coupled with deep concern for the children—needed help and needed it immediately. It was clear that not just the young people and teachers in these schools but young people and teachers and parents throughout the New York area and across the country were profoundly affected by the events of September 11.

School librarians and public librarians who work with young people are not professional counselors, but they are skilled in selecting and evaluating information and resources in many print and electronic formats for students themselves and for their teachers and families and skilled in promoting their independent use; in other words, they serve important support for and other roles in counseling. With this immediate and urgent need for information and resources, librarians and other information professionals can contribute by retrieving and evaluating information and resources in two different yet complementary areas. The most immediate need is for information and resources to help make sense of the event itself, the tragic deaths, and the context for the attacks and their aftermath (and some useful websites supporting this have already developed).[51]

The events of September 11 followed less than two years after the shooting of students and teachers at Columbine High School by two classmates. In that instance, the unthinkable happened in a school—much of it in the school's library. Would kids ever feel safe in school or a library again? More importantly, could kids treat any perceived "outsider" among them with understanding? Librarians helped students by identifying and evaluating resources that promoted understanding and by putting those resources into student hands as soon as possible. The events of September 11 have shaken the very foundation of the lives of young people. As teachers and parents cope with helping their students and their children, librarians can work collaboratively with them to provide the resources and information for understanding and solace, and information science schools where many of the future librarians are educated need to reevaluate their role in how they prepare these professionals for their careers and unexpected events such as what occurred on September 11. These events can provide our students a significant case study to build their competencies in the retrieval, evaluation, and use of information and resources in all formats that can be of real and immediate benefit to young people, their teachers, and their parents.

Ethics, Policies, Responsibilities, and Rights in the Post-9/11 World

While many people watched television for long periods, there was also a significant increase in the use of other media, especially radio, newspapers (both print and online), and magazines. How the story was told by the different media, why individuals relied on some forms rather than others, and what the implications are of these uses are among the research questions needing to be addressed by faculty and their students at schools of information science. The incessant television, radio, and other media coverage of the September 11 events has burned into our minds the graphic images of and voices related to the hijacked planes' attacks, the collapse of the World Trade Center, the victims of the attacks struggling to escape, the efforts by rescuers to find the injured, and the subsequent investigations into who carried out the attacks. Not long after the terrorist attacks, all of the major television news networks agreed to review videos prepared by bin Laden and his network before airing them because of concerns about the content and even coded messages. This was an unprecedented agreement, one justified by one network executive (Andrew Hayward, CBS News president) because "this is a new situation, a new war and a new kind of enemy. Given the historic events we're enmeshed in, it's appropriate to explore new ways of fulfilling our responsibilities to the public."[52] This agreement also raises, of course, considerable concerns about television news coverage and access to news information.

Much of the media coverage has been chilling and some of it has raised concerns about the role of the Fourth Estate in reporting on such events (a topic that has long been discussed by many commentators on society, public policy, and other areas).[53] If anything the journalistic coverage of these events demonstrates that information is not merely a neutral element in our society. We must reevaluate America's position on legislating taste and enabling public access to certain forms of information. Diversity must be allowed to influence the study of the ethics of information. Many questions have been raised concerning why some individuals and groups hate America so much, what their objections to their perceptions of Americans' lifestyles are, how "norms" of taste and "common values" vary among countries and groups, and how diverse opinions and views influence definitions and understandings of ethics. These and other related questions need to be addressed, especially in schools with a high percentage of international students (as is the case with many of the information science schools in North America).

For years other professional schools have been considering how areas like ethics and more humanistic aspects of the uses of technologies need to be included in their educational programs. Our school was a pioneer in introducing information ethics, starting with a lecture series, and then introducing a course (in one term also a doctoral seminar), a website, and a fellow's program. Ethical issues are also addressed in many other courses as well, and an examination is needed to determine how these issues can be addressed in other courses and what courses should be cross-listed. In the archives and records-management specialization, for example, there has been a course on "Archival Access and Advocacy" considering similar matters such as the ethics of access, the accountability of records for organizations and society, and case studies documenting the impact of open or restricted access on particular societal groups. The introductory core course in the Master's of Library and Information Science (MLIS) degree program, Understanding Information, also provides some orientation to such concerns. Faculty should consider whether the orientation of undergraduate and graduate students to ethical issues is satisfactory. Other information science schools need to evaluate how ethical dimensions are integrated into their curriculum. Faculty should consider how best to orient both undergraduate and graduate students to information ethics and to related ethical issues. Intertwined with information ethics are the areas of information and telecommunications policy.

Among key policy issues that have been included and must continue to be addressed are those related to privacy, access (including "digital divide" concerns), the protection of rights of intellectual property owners and users, and security. Again, these have been the subject of many scholars and have generally been featured in courses in information science schools.[54] Both rights and responsibilities of the stakeholders are considered, and it is evident that the interests of various stakeholders around the world are often in conflict. Balancing these interests, especially security and privacy protection, in the aftermath of the terrorists' attacks is challenging. One early commentator on the media coverage of the September 11 events reflects on television coverage going back to the Vietnam con-

flict and notes: "In our innocence [during the Vietnam War], we
thought we were the real reporters; television was show business.
But we were seeing a new kind of asymmetrical war, in which the
weaker side on the ground bypasses the stronger, exploiting technology to impact directly on hearts and minds on the other side. No
one wrote about that, and television, the least self-critical of media,
still hasn't grasped how easily it can be hijacked by terrorists."[55]
Such a statement suggests that an information science school is not
only teaching about how to build and run information systems or
how to use and preserve information, but it is also trying to instill
into its students a critical sense of how to evaluate these systems and
sources. Lest we become too self-critical, this same veteran news-
man ends his commentary by noting, "And these dry words, published a week after the event, are too soon to possess historical authority, too late to advise caution before the images have soaked into
our collective memories. Nevertheless, it's worth noting the de-
fenselessness of great cities before determined attackers. Recall
those axe-wielding barbarians, our own ancestors, who turned the
opulent cities of the late Roman empire into uninhabitable ruins.
Jutes, Saxons, Vandals and the rest had no television, or even writing, only word of mouth to spread terror. It was quite enough."[56]

Some of these challenges will require that faculty in information
science schools not only look outward for examples and case studies about such policy and ethical issues, but it also seems to be the
case that the aftermath of the September 11 events has thrown university faculty themselves into a more critical light about how they
can discuss such controversial and critical issues and sustain free
speech when they are themselves sharply divided about the United
States' role and response. Stanley Kurtz recently wrote, "Most of the
criticism leveled at professors in the wake of the September 11 attacks has come not from other faculty members, but from students,
administrators, and media commentators. Among faculty members
themselves, there has been little real debate on the causes of this war.
That fact, more than any other, explains why recent condemnations
of professorial opinion have sometimes gone so far as to challenge
or contravene our traditions of free speech. If the professorate was
diverse enough to allow for an authentic debate over the causes of
the war; if our tradition of free speech had not for years been under
challenge as a mere cover for the oppressive power of the social
elites; if we had not been so recently subjected to codes, written and

unwritten, in which sensitivity trumped free speech; then we would now have far less to fear from the pent-up anger of students, administrators, or the public over controversial comments about the war."⁵⁷ Focused on information science issues and the education of future information professionals, we might need to be studying ourselves (and to a certain extent, faculty in such schools have been doing this as they introduce and revise courses in such areas as the sociology of information or understanding information). We probably should have been doing this more strenuously long before now.

Information and Other Security Issues

Information science educators also need to be watching others, as well. Politicians, journalists, and public-policy experts and human-rights advocates almost immediately began discussing needs for increased security in airline and other travel, surveillance to counteract terrorism, and other mechanisms related to matters such as granting student visas, hiring for jobs with potential security implications at places like airports, and other activities with important implications for personal privacy and rights. One commentator on these issues notes, "There is no doubt that the nation is in a new era," with a "shift in balance to security over privacy."⁵⁸ Within a few days of the September 11 attacks, the Bush administration was moving to roll back former restrictions on activities such as wiretapping, generating quick responses from civil-rights groups worrying about the efforts to make changes so quickly without serious deliberation by Congress. James X. Dempsey of the Center for Democracy and Technology argues, "Some of these proposals would seem to involve a fundamental rewriting of the wiretap laws." Rather, Dempsey stated, "We need deliberate, open scrutiny by the legislative process." Laura W. Murphy of the American Civil Liberties Union had a similar response: "We cannot let our grief and anger overwhelm our democracy. Now is the time for the people's representatives to be even more thoughtful and deliberative than usual."⁵⁹ Ethical and policy questions, often interrelated, were raised throughout the United States and in other countries, as well.

The most obvious and dramatic legislative effort (at least so far) was the Combating Terrorism Act of 2001, an amendment to an appropriations bill passed by the Senate on September 13, with a controversial section allowing the government to capture information related to a suspect's activities in cyberspace. A version of this bill ultimately passed and was signed into law. Stewart Baker, head of the technology practice at Steptoe & Johnson, a Washington, D.C., law firm, and former general counsel of the National Security Agency, notes that this would allow the government to obtain a list of "everyone you send e-mail to, when you sent it, who replied to you, how long the messages were, whether they had attachments, as well as where you went online." Some argue that this allows more information gathering than any other provision in government at present.[60] Moving quickly in reacting to the terrorist acts, the antiterrorist legislation seems to have implications going far beyond terrorist threats. A *Business Week* reporter ascertains that "Hackers, virus-writers and web site defacers would face life imprisonment without the possibility of parole under legislation proposed by the Bush Administration that would classify most computer crimes as acts of terrorism." This reporter concludes, "Most of the terrorism offenses are violent crimes, or crimes involving chemical, biological, or nuclear weapons. But the list also includes the provisions of the Computer Fraud and Abuse Act that make it illegal to crack a computer for the purpose of obtaining anything of value, or to deliberately cause damage. Likewise, launching a malicious program that harms a system, like a virus, or making an extortionate threat to damage a computer are included in the definition of terrorism."[61]

New bills are being introduced almost daily in both houses of the U.S. Congress, and the administration's views are being observed in strategies to preclude votes from taking place on either of the latest two bills. One recent effort (at the time of writing this essay) is a push for a "pre-conference" which means that House and Senate staff and key members would meet behind closed doors to get the House to accept provisions of the Senate bill, thus obviating the need for a conference. Several efforts for compromise are under way, but these may not reach the floor in either chamber.

Not only do these recommendations and ideas have implications regarding traditional rights such as privacy, but they also have implications for the uses of information technology with suggestions for things like the issuance of smart cards: "Such cards, with computer chips, would have detailed information about those they were issued to and would identify them when read by a computer. The cards could be coordinated with fingerprints or, in a few years, facial characteristics, and be programmed to permit or limit access through turnstiles to buildings or areas. They could track someone's location, financial transactions, criminal history and even driving speed on a particular highway on a given night." Obviously, this would mean an entirely new era of surveillance unlike anything the United States has faced.[62] Proposals for such identity cards have already drawn protests in Great Britain and Australia.[63]

On the other hand, these smart-card technologies, as envisioned in the medical-informatics community, offer a powerful assistance to emergency medical workers. As those who survived the harrowing attacks were dispersed to medical centers and burn specialty units in New York and New Jersey they were often separated from their personal medical histories, their health-insurance records, and their emergency contacts. Smart cards, presently being pilot tested by a number of health-care providers and insurers, might have offered information otherwise unavailable to EMTs and ER staff. Increasingly, information science schools offer the opportunity for students to study medical informatics, and its subspecialities in electronic patient records, bioterrorism surveillance systems, and consumer informatics. The situation generated by the events of September 11 offers a new and positive concept to explore this technology. The reactions to information technologies such as smart cards, ranging from criticisms by civil libertarians to advocacy by health-care professionals, reflect how complex information machinery can be in societal applications and the need for information science schools to explore how their students can be better oriented to such a wide range of uses and discussion.

Such schools need to reconsider just how effectively they are dealing with such threats to personal and societal freedoms, especially regarding the use of information technologies and even dealing with their own students. The events of September 11 might cause, for example, a tightening of access to government information that was already being restricted. Bruce Craig of the National Coordinating Committee for the Promotion of History recently reported that the Central Intelligence Agency was pressuring State Department officials to "destroy the inventory of 1,500 copies of volume XVI of the *Foreign Relations of the United States* (FRUS) series dealing with US policy towards Greece, Cyprus, and Turkey during the 1960s and to replace it with a sanitized version." The reason given is that this volume contains a "handful of documents that allude to CIA intervention in the electoral process in Greece some 35 years ago. CIA officials claim that release of such documents could upset current relations with Greece or even provide a pretext for terrorism."[64] Also quickly after the terrorist bombings, Attorney General John D. Ashcroft issued a new Freedom of Information Act (FOIA) policy statement directing federal agency heads to be cautious releasing records to journalists and others, citing national security.[65] Citizens advocacy groups, such as OMB Watch, have created special websites to document what kinds of information we are being blocked from in the new intensified environment of the war on terrorism.[66]

Such allusions to potential terrorism might also provide an opportunity for the federal government to restrict information in unprecedented ways because of Congress's and the public's concerns for safety. Colleges and universities were also being asked to reveal normally confidential information about their students to federal agencies such as the FBI, and given the nature of information science schools it is expected that students in these schools also will be targeted.[67] This is additional evidence that information science schools can use their own institutions to try to understand some of the more complicated matters regarding the creation, use, and maintenance of information.

The terrorist attacks also brought heightened concern about computer viruses, security, and hacking. Reports about both how the terrorists had used the Internet and the investigators were tracing their steps also appeared. The terrorists apparently used computers in public libraries in an effort to cover their tracks.[68] Within days of the events, information technology experts were being consulted about the implications of technology supporting terrorist and antiterrorist activities. The *New York Times*, for example, brought together six experts to discuss these issues: Ray Kurzweil, an expert in artificial intelligence; Peter Neumann, an expert on security; Bruce Sterling, a science-fiction author and writer on technology; Lawrence Lessig, a law professor; Severo Ornstein, a hardware engineer who worked on the original Arpanet; and Whitfield Diffie, the inventor of public-key cryptography. Their discussion about the implications of technology on the September 11 events was far ranging and featured many differing opinions, but also attested to the value of bringing together such diverse expertise on the complex causes and results of the terrorist attacks.[69] Because of their mission and history, information science schools also can draw on such expertise from among their own faculty, especially to consider the role of the Internet/World Wide Web. Such schools include engineers, librarians, archivists, historians, psychologists, and a wide array of other disciplines. Some of these schools also feature interdisciplinary connections across the campus enabling them to examine an event such as what occurred on September 11 in a multiplicity of ways.

Computer security is certainly one aspect of the kinds of programs offered at an information science school, like ours, that has grabbed more media and public attention, in a way that is perhaps far more lasting than all the Y2K concerns. Bruce Schneier devoted a special issue of his newsletter *Crypto-Gram* to the September 11 events. In it he writes, among other things, the following: "Computer security experts have a lot of expertise that can be applied to the real world. First and foremost, we have well-developed senses of what security looks like. We can tell the difference between real security and snake oil. And the new airport security rules, put in place after September 11, look and smell a whole lot like snake oil."[70] Such discussions represent opportunities for faculty and student research not just about the technical aspects of security and related concerns but about what separates real solutions of lasting use from rhetoric and political posturing. The events of September 11 provide ample opportunity for case studies for teaching about how to distinguish snake oil and workable, practical approaches.

Beyond computer security are issues of information security. While it is critical to protect computer networks and systems, it is also essential to protect information content from invasion, corruption, and distortion. The protection of the integrity of information and the privacy of individuals is an area of great interest to information science schools that offer courses in different areas such as medical information, library records, electronic government, and others. The role of governments at all levels in creating, gathering, organizing, managing, preserving, and disseminating information is increasingly important, especially for disaster preparedness, health care, and informing the public about the actions of government. E-government is one of the most rapidly growing and important domains within KM and will deserve ever greater attention in the future.

Economics of Information

One of the long-term implications of the World Trade Center destruction relates to the economic health of American high-tech companies. Before the attack many of these companies were facing economic problems, and the events of September 11 added disruptions because of shipping problems, travel restrictions reducing sales efforts, and other similar problems. While there may be a temporary increase in business due to the needs to replace destroyed computers, the manufacturers of semiconductors, microchips, and computers all face difficult times ahead according to industry analysts.[71]

The destruction of the World Trade Center and attack on the Pentagon highlight the vulnerability of any major company, government agency, or academic institution. The loss of life, of course, is always the main concern. However, other major organization resources are lost as well, not the least of which is the knowledge of those lost and the information and internal information services that are destroyed as well. Faculties of schools of information sciences have done numerous studies of the economics of information and information services in organizations.[72] These studies have focused on the usefulness and value of information and information services, as well as their effects on organization goals, productivity, and profitability (where appropriate). It is abundantly clear that the disappearance of these resources can have a devastating, if not fatal, effect on any organization. This is true even if only one site of a multisite organization is involved. The economic implications of the loss of knowledge and information extend well beyond any one organization to the local community and to the nation. Some of our economic studies have focused on those higher-order effects of the economics of information.

Given the current health of the American economy it is obvious that information science schools will focus more on the economics of information. These schools have often been seen as advocates for the acquisition of new technologies. Nicholson Baker, in his diatribe about American library preservation, points to these schools as a principal source of the problem in producing professionals who are more interested in creating technocrats committed to playing with high-tech toys and solutions than in devising ways of maintaining the resources of our cultural heritage housed in libraries and archives. Other information technologists have examined the claims made about computers and found them coming up far short of what they are purported to support.[73] The situation is, of course, more complicated than this simple characterization. The events of September 11 reflect a complex society in which international events, global politics, the stock market, terrorists, government, and the media all have profound implications for what information profession-als do and how they are educated for their positions. Economics of information production, management, and use will need to assume a more central place in the curriculum of all kinds of information professionals.

Memorializing and Documenting Violent Events and Their Aftermath

As the events of September 11 unfolded, discussions ensued about how these events would be or should be remembered and under-stood. The role of records and public memory has been both an im-portant area of scholarship and a feature of some information sci-ence schools, especially those with archives, history of the book, and related programs. Memory can be considered an aspect of both in-formation and evidence systems, and records and information sys-tems certainly play critical roles in how sources are created and ulti-mately made available for future memory purposes. University library collections are often referred to as repositories of knowledge, archives are often seen as having functions comparable to museums, and information scientists refer to memory needs in both technical (memory capacities of computers) and more cultural (the World Wide Web as memory of the world) ways. While information scien-tists might look at the problem in most practical ways—Stewart Brand notes that "digital storage is easy; digital preservation is hard"[74]—the nature of the terrorist attacks complicate the situation even more. Now we are not just concerned with rescuing data from the destruction sites, but we are concerned with how, or whether, we should memorialize the sites.[75] And memorializing battles of the new Information Age war poses new challenges *and* opportunities because of the nature of the events and the documentary sources cre-ated of these events (this is discussed more fully in the next section on the Internet and its role).

Observers of the events of September 11 were quick to begin thinking about the long-term implications of understanding the destruction of the World Trade Center. The New York State Archives and Records Administration, located a few hours away in Albany but with regional networks located in New York City and adjacent areas, announced plans to try to document the tragedy through the records of state government agencies involved as both victims and agents of rescue and recovery, local governments, and

nongovernmental organizations and institutions (such as charita-
ble, social, religious, and political agencies).[76] The events of September 11 also were documented by moving images in unprecedented ways. The video of the first plane attack was captured by
two French documentary filmmakers who happened to be in the
World Trade Center area working on another project. The story
about this starts, "Being in the wrong place at the right time has led
a documentary filmmaker to record what may be to the September
11 terrorist attack what the Zapruder film was to the Kennedy assassination."[77] A number of writers also wrote about the film images of the World Trade Center destruction and considered how,
for many people, these images were reminiscent of Hollywood disaster films.[78]

Such topics can fit comfortably within an information science
school. At our own school, the archives and records-management
specialization has focused on public memory for some years, leading to dissertations, articles, and courses with such an emphasis. Recently, I presented papers, along with those of four of my current or
former doctoral students, at the Society of American Archivists' annual conference on archives and memory, and they are now collab-
orating on a lengthy article exploring this area. This emphasis has
included both societal and organizational memory, and the afore-
mentioned KM area also needs to include a focus on organizational
memory. Information technology courses have often focused on
technical aspects of machine memory as well, and this provides another means by which to consider the various implications of memory. Faculty in our own school might consider various ways they
have been teaching about aspects of memory and how these relate
to the aftermath of the World Trade Center destruction.

Earlier in this chapter we considered the matter of workplaces and
the question of whether the World Trade Center buildings would need
to be reconstructed or not, given the differences in technologies now
involved in fabricating such structures. This reemerges in a discussion
of memory. The World Trade Center was attacked and destroyed as the
result of its being a symbol of Western capitalism and a global economy. However, when the World Trade Center was originally constructed it was controversial and not universally loved or appreci-
ated.[79] This certainly impacts on the issue of memorialization. At the
least, it suggests how a building passes through stages of public recog-
nition and can be changed quickly by events affecting it. A school of in-

formation science has the ability to consider the nature, role, context, and value of memory from the technical to the cultural.

The Internet and Its Role

One of the most obvious aspects of the events of September 11 was the role of the Internet/World Wide Web in providing information about what was happening and even being a device for those planning and carrying out the attacks. The search engine Google reported that on September 11 searching for news-related content increased by a factor of sixty.[80] Studies are beginning to appear about how Listservs and other Internet resources are being used to respond to other disasters,[81] and it is likely we will see a number of such studies related to the events of September 11. A curricular case study in the use of the Internet by medical librarians is already under preparation by Ellen Detlefsen, one of our school's faculty. Within a day of the attack, practicing medical librarians were sharing, via their e-list called MEDLIB-L, resource lists of materials such as on the forensic identification from burned remains, bioterrorism resources for hospital preparedness and public-health planning, consumer health resources in English and in Spanish for post-traumatic stress, and the availability of verified websites for locating World Trade Center survivors in metro New York and New Jersey hospitals. The shared resources and collective professional knowledge brought together information specialists from as close to the World Trade Center as the New York Academy of Medicine, and as far away as a naval hospital on Guam. Such efforts provide opportunities for faculty and students to work together on research studies and in building case studies for future teaching.

Even before the attacks, however, it was obvious that the web was a venue where one could read directly the statements of those who were thought to have planned and carried out the attacks. Many of the basic texts and principles of Osama bin Laden are readily available on the web, providing the unique opportunity for individuals to go around the news reports and interpretations and to go straight to the primary documents in a way the public has not generally had the opportunity to do.[82] Because of the importance of the web, shortly after the attacks, Brewster Kahle announced that the Internet Archive, in collaboration with Alexa Internet, SUNY, Library of Congress, and the University of Washington, was archiving pages and sites relating to the terrorist attacks in New York and the District of Columbia in order "to make sure there is a solid historical record of this time."[83] Other scholars determined that Americans' responses to the attacks were being documented in unique ways via the World Wide Web, and these scholars started to build archives of aspects of relief or support being provided by sites on the web.[84] A *Washington Post* reporter starts an article about this in the following manner: "Minutes after suicide planes crashed into the World Trade Center and opened a hole in the American psyche, researchers began capturing electronic snapshots of how the world was responding via the World Wide Web." In this article Kahle is quoted as saying that this effort to document the September 11 events on the web is part of "trying to build . . . a new kind of library." Diane Kresh, the Library of Congress's director of public-service collections is also quoted: "We think the Internet is absolutely as important as print media for these events. Why? Because the Internet is immediate, far-reaching and reaches a variety of audiences. You have everything from self-styled experts to known experts commenting and giving their spin."[85] Not only does the role of the World Wide Web fall squarely within the research interests of the information science faculties, but such research can be carried out remotely far from the scenes of disaster in New York City and Washington, D.C.

Preservation

Information science schools have long featured an emphasis on preservation management, often building on the established archives and records-management curriculum. The events of September 11 also have drawn new attention to preservation issues, in addition to matters like disaster preparedness. A number of New York City area museums, archives, and libraries were affected by the massive destruction at the World Trade Center site. A report on this aspect of the terrorist attacks notes, "By one count, in New York City there are 42 museums, 57 libraries and archives, and some 245 outdoor sculptures that possibly have been touched by recent events." The report continues, "The greatest continuing threat in New York is the dust and ash from debris that still blankets much of the city. The National Museum of the American Indian (located just a few blocks from Ground Zero), for example, is covered in a few inches of ash. Reportedly, the dust is granular and greasy and may scratch delicate surfaces. Untold number of books, delicate fabrics, historic photographs and prints, as well as art works may need careful cleaning and conservation."[86] The library at the Pentagon also was badly damaged and several of its staff members injured, and the rebuilding of this library operation also includes some serious preservation challenges.[87] The United States Customs Service also lost all of its reference libraries at the World Trade Center site.

Already, for example, the World Trade Center destruction has generated some interest in long-existing standards related to records and information systems. The Association of Information and Image Managers (AIIM) offered, at no charge, use of its standards on materials related to disaster recovery and preparedness such as on the quality assurance and preservation of microfilm, optical disks, and records requiring legal acceptance.[88] While preservation and archives courses draw students' attention to these and other standards, it is important that information science schools reexamine this and other parts of the curriculum to ensure that students learn about standards supporting the continuing use and protection of information and records systems. Long before the events of September 11, information technologists had been questioning issues of the longevity of information in digital form.[89]

The tragic events of September 11 also serve to sharpen the focus on questions concerning the importance of conservation and preservation efforts, coming as they did only a few months after the publication of Nicholson Baker's *Double Fold*. From the standpoint of library and information science education, where educators have long been preoccupied with questions concerning the core knowledge of the field and the transmittal of such knowledge through the core curriculum of MLIS programs, recent events and broader trends (in the management of research collections and the interest in digitizing research materials) suggest that it may now be reasonable, if not necessary, for these educators to consider placing preservation as a major element within the framework of their core curricula.

Organization and access (or cataloging and reference, for readers less fond of the fashionably oblique terminology that characterizes much of contemporary library and information science education) have long been viewed as the most fundamental concerns of the field, and that view has tended to form the larger part of the professional curricula. In recent times, there has been a tendency to revise that orientation in core curricula by way of expansion, as the audience to which library and information science education addresses itself fragments, and as external factors, including competition in the information marketplace, begin to reshape what is regarded as essential knowledge. The first response has been to emphasize information technology and management, but it may well be that a second round of responses will be focused more sharply on those areas of professional knowledge and skill that are genuinely distinguishing. Given that archivists and librarians stand almost alone in the assumption of responsibility for maintaining the integrity and continuity of the historical and literary record, and in view of the increasingly popular perception that this is a responsibility of the first order, it seems reasonable to imagine that preservation will move to the center of the MLIS curriculum. It is, moreover, not merely a response to tragedy and loss. As the digital realm evolves, questions are being raised about the functional roles that archivists and librarians will play in the future, and while exacting answers are yet to appear, it may be safe to presume that the primary roles may be defined by the functional areas in which their collective expertise is most distinctive and least duplicated; namely, in the areas of information organization and preservation.

Perhaps these events will pull together the information science faculty who possess greatly varying expertise, ranging from software and hardware issues to those who consider more the cultural, social, and humanistic aspects of the uses of information and information technologies. Over the past twenty years, especially, these schools and related professional associations have wrestled with, debated, and even split over such different perspectives. Electronic records management, digital libraries and digital preservation, and other concerns have brought forth an immense body of literature (too extensive even to try to summarize here), much of it calling for greater cooperation and different approaches. The destruction of the World Trade Center and damage to the Pentagon, along with the loss of records, libraries, and artifacts might stimulate a renewed interest in cooperative efforts. Information science schools seem to be a logical focal point for such efforts, since they already have many different types of expertise on their faculties, a research infrastructure, and a need to provide relevant teaching of future information professionals.

CONCLUSION: FINAL PRACTICAL THOUGHTS

Throughout this essay we have considered how the transformation of the world on September 11 impacts on the curriculum and programs of information science schools. Much of this discussion has stressed needs to rethink both these schools' curriculum and opportunities for service to the communities and constituencies they serve. As difficult as it may be to consider, the events of September 11 are providing some new attention on the kinds of academic and continuing-education programs information science schools offer and this may translate to new avenues for recruiting, grant funding, and other activities, counterbalancing other potential negative impacts (such as the loss of international students with limits on student visas and foreign students going home because of fears about their safety).[90]

For this and other reasons, information science schools' faculty need to consider the ramifications of the terrorist attacks on September 11 and events yet to come. The varied expertise and experience of these faculties can be harnessed to deal with such matters, ranging from reconsideration of their academic programs to research and publication. As information science faculty we must do more than just write about these concerns. We envision that we will undertake reviews of the curricula to determine how best to address these issues; we will explore opportunities for research and development projects to answer some of the questions raised; and we will work with the wider community on service projects to effect some of the changes needed.

The most immediate matters may concern just how information science schools teach, the kinds of positions they prepare their students for, and how, as a result, they determine their mission. All of the attention about the destruction of records and other information systems led to an upsurge of interest in the management of personal and individual documents.[91] How do we integrate personal record keeping into our normal focus on organizational systems?[92]

There are many ways we can sum up the far-reaching consequences of the tragic events of September 11 for information science schools. Will we see new kinds of jobs for our graduates? Will these positions require new kinds of courses and delivery of these courses to new kinds of students? Will we see new kinds of students coming into these schools?

We need to reimagine the kinds of jobs we are educating our students for, anticipating that the market for these graduates may change in fundamental ways. For example, our own school has supported the development of one of the leading North American programs in archives and records management. While this program has evolved to support students focusing on records and record-keeping systems, the majority of students attracted to this program have come here to prepare themselves for positions in very traditional archival programs (historical societies, museums, colleges and universities, and government agencies) in very traditional positions (archivists, records managers, and manuscripts librarians).

As a result, the curriculum for this archives and records-management program supports such career objectives as well as it can. However, it is likely that a new kind of archivist or records manager may be called upon in the future, one more oriented to issues of accountability and current use of records than to the maintenance of long-term records for future historical research. Minimally, the archives and records-management courses must be reconfigured to support positions where professionals are concentrated on disaster preparedness, recovery, and other similar functions. This means that the courses must try to become more interdisciplinary but not in a manner usually considered by the archives and records-management communities, where they draw on history, legal, and other disciplines long connected to archival studies. We need to attract nonarchivists, individuals who look at such issues from technical and policy perspectives rather than cultural or historical viewpoints, into the classrooms with future archivists in order to prepare these future professionals for the complex and perhaps different roles they may be encountering. This may require a renewed consideration of the use of distance education for the delivery of courses, a teaching approach that has not been widely embraced in this discipline in North America.

Thinking about new curricular programs or revisions in present ones might mean pressing information science schools to be more innovative in how they support teaching. In the past, even in the most comprehensive of these schools, faculties have tended to cluster around a particular degree program, like the Master's in Library Science or the Master's in Information Science, without much need or incentive to cross over disciplinary boundaries. Now we need a new kind of interdisciplinarity, similar to what some have been predicting or calling for in higher education for years, where faculty move in and out of courses, team teaching, guest lecturing, crossing departmental and disciplinary boundaries to work with each other and to serve on doctoral and other commitments, and so forth.[93] We might have expected that this sort of thing would have been occurring with the debate about the future of the printed book and the rise of digital libraries and e-books, but while the scholarship on the book has grown and become more diversified, this issue has not galvanized such schools. Some more recent commentators have noted that the debate about the future of the book is really a false debate since we need to be concerned with "*all* modes of knowledge, for in the end they are complementary, not antithetical."[94] At the least, however, we still need to bring the debate into the classroom because it energizes critical thinking about the roles of information professionals.[95] It is the magnitude of the destruction of the World Trade Center and the Pentagon and the ensuing war on terrorism that might provide the necessary impetus for radical new thinking and programmatic responses.

There may be other ways of dealing with such matters, such as in developing innovative lecture series where outside experts, representing a variety of perspectives not normally present in such schools, could be brought in for public lectures and planned interaction with both faculty and students. The physical presence of such experts would be welcome, but these schools should also explore the greater use of distance education and web-based technologies to bring these individuals into the classrooms in ways that could enhance focusing on the kinds of complex issues generated by the new war against international terrorism. Government experts, civil-liberties critics, and experts on topics as wide-ranging as the Islamic faith and Middle Eastern and Western attitudes towards information technologies could make these schools' programs much more meaningful in a world that is simultaneously becoming more complex as well as reliant on information networks, the media, and other related technologies.

Library schools, the ancestors of information science schools, have often not been seen as innovative, but as traditional enclaves for traditional-thinking faculty and professions. A decade ago, these schools were under pressure from university administrators to justify their existence in higher education, and a number were closed, apparently because they did not connect to the university's mission and because they often had not built relationships with other schools and academic units.⁹⁶ Now these schools have the opportunity to lead in reacting to and studying many of the aspects of the new Information Age war. In a provocative book about information technology and higher education, James O'Donnell, a classicist, wonders about what the future roles of specialized faculty will be. "Can we imagine a time in our universities when librarians are the well-paid principals and teachers their mere acolytes? I do not think we can or should rule out that possibility." He pushes the point even more: "The real roles of the professor in an information-rich world will be not to provide information but to advise, guide, and encourage students wading through the deep waters of the information flood. Professors in this environment will thrive as mentors, tutors, backseat drivers, and coaches."⁹⁷ The events of September 11, 2001, may move information science schools into a much more critical position within universities and society than they have ever before held. Or, if these schools ignore the implications and try to consider business as usual, they may become more marginalized than ever before.

The world, including that in which information science schools reside, has changed dramatically in a very brief period of time.

NOTES

1. "The Day the World Changed," *Economist*, September 15–21, 2001, 13.

2. Stanley Hoffman, "On the War," *New York Review of Books*, November 1, 2001, at www.nybooks.com/articles/14660 (accessed October 9, 2001).

3. Lewis H. Lapham, "Drums along the Potomac: New War, Old Music," *Harper's Magazine* 303 (November 2001): 39.

4. Jeffrey L. Pasley, "And Now for Something Completely Similar," *Common-Place* 2 (October 2001), at www.common-place.org/publicj/200110.shtml (accessed October 1, 2001).

5. See, for example, James A. Dewar, "The Information Age and the Printing Press: Looking Backward to See Ahead," *Ubiquity* 25 (August 15–21, 2000), at www.acm.org/ubiquity/views/j_dewar_1.html. Using Elizabeth Eisenstein's history of the printing press, Dewar, a senior mathematician at RAND, suggests that there are "compelling" parallels between the printing-press era and the contemporary Information Age. He concludes that there will be "changes in the information age . . . as dramatic as those in the Middle Ages in Europe," the "future of the information age will be dominated by unintended

consequences," "it will be decades before we see the full effects of the information age," and "the above factors combine to argue for: a) keeping the Internet unregulated, and b) taking a much more experimental approach to information policy." Read Richard J. Cox's response, "The Information Age and History: Looking Backward to See Us," *Ubiquity* 30 (September 26–October 4, 2000), at www.acm.org/ubiquity/.

6. See Paul N. Edwards, *The Closed World: Computers and the Politics of Discourse in Cold War America* (Cambridge, Mass.: MIT Press, 1996) and Martin Campbell-Kelly and William Aspray, *Computer: A History of the Information Machine* (New York: Basic Books, 1996).

7. Todd Lappin, "Preserving the Voices of the Twin Towers," *New York Times*, October 11, 2001, at www.nytimes.com/2001/10/11/technology/circuits/11AUDI.html?ex=1003818852&ei=1&en=2fe8ef7f2a036885 (accessed October 12, 2001).

8. See, for example, Social Sciences Department, Carnegie Library of Pittsburgh, "Resources on Terrorist Attack on America," at www.carnegielibrary.org/clp/Socsci/ROTA.html with bibliographies, information about emergency and related services, news articles, speeches and interviews, eyewitness accounts, images, resources for dealing with tragic events, and other useful materials. The New York State Historical Records Advisory Board and the New York State Archives established a "World Trade Center Disaster Recovery" website with information about the status of repositories in the affected area, list of federal, state, and local agencies affected by the disaster, resources for businesses recovering from the disaster, technical and financial assistance resources, and other information about documenting the events of September 11. The website is www.nyshrab.org/WTC/wtc.html. The Library of Congress also has established the "September 11, 2001, Documentary Project" at lcweb.loc.gov/folklife/nineeleven/nineelevenhome.html. This project is described as follows: "The American Folklife Center at the Library of Congress is calling upon folklorists and other ethnographers across the nation to document on recordings the thoughts and feelings expressed by average citizens following the tragic events of September 11, 2001. These recordings and other documentation materials will become part of the Center's Archive of Folk Culture where they will be preserved and made available to future generations. The Center will collect and preserve the audio-taped interviews and supporting materials that present the personal experience stories of average Americans in the wake of the terrorist attack. In addition, the Center will collect photographic documentation of the memorial tributes that have sprung up near the Pentagon and at the site of the World Trade Center disaster. These temporary memorials include posters, photographs, flowers, flags, and other memorabilia through which those connected to the disaster victims and others express their grief and sympathy."

9. For example, the U.S. Customs Service lost a specialized library used by its agents to classify imports in the destruction of the World Trade Center.

10. "The Day the World Changed," 14.

11. David Ronfeldt and John Arquilla, "Networks, Netwars, and the Fight for the Future," *First Monday* 6 (October 2001), at firstmonday.org /issues/issue6_10/ronfeldt/index.html (accessed October 5, 2001).

12. Seymour M. Hersh, "Annals of National Security: What Went Wrong; The C.I.A. and the Failure of American Intelligence," *New Yorker*, October 10, 2001, at newyorker.com/FACT/. The connection of information professionals like librarians to the CIA and Cold War intelligence approaches has recently been put into the limelight as part of a conspiracy and loss of public trust by Nicholson Baker, *Double Fold: Libraries and the Assault on Paper* (New York: Random House, 2001). I have written a response to Baker's book, *Vandals in the Stacks? A Response to Nicholson Baker's Assault on Libraries* (Westport, Conn.: Greenwood Press, 2002).

13. Ronfeldt and Arquilla, "Networks, Netwars, and the Fight for the Future."

14. For some perceptive discussion of such matters, see Daniel C. Hallin, *The 'Uncensored War': The Media and Vietnam* (Berkeley: University of California Press, 1989); Susan D. Moeller, *Shooting War: Photography and the American Experience of Combat* (New York: Basic Books, Inc., 1989); and Barbie Zelizer, *Remembering to Forget: Holocaust Memory through the Camera's Eye* (Chicago: University of Chicago Press, 1998).

15. "Picture Perfect?" *Economist*, October 20, 2001, 75.

16. Ana Marie Cox, "The Changed Classroom, Post-September 11," *Chronicle of Higher Education*, October 26, 2001, A16-A18.

17. Katherine S. Mangan, "Terrorist Attacks Prompt Professional Schools to Add New Training," *Chronicle of Higher Education*, October 26, 2001, A18. Professional schools mentioned included public health, medicine, nursing, law, business and economics, engineering, and security studies.

18. See, for example, Paul Hoyningen-Huene, *Constructing Scientific Revolutions: Thomas S. Kuhn's Philosophy of Science* (Chicago: University of Chicago Press, 1993).

19. Dan Carnevale, "Congress is Urged to Spend More on Research into Ways to Counter Cyberterrorism," *Chronicle of Higher Education*, October 11, 2001, at chronicle.com/free/2001/10/2001101101t.htm (accessed October 12, 2001).

20. There has been considerable discussion for more than thirty years about the emergence, viability, and desirability of the "paperless" office. For a recent discussion, refer to Abigail J. Sellen and Richard H. R. Harper, *The Myth of the Paperless Office* (Cambridge, Mass.: MIT Press, 2002). For a convenient summary of recent research, see Ann Balough, "How Paper Facilitates the Way People Work," *Records & Information Management Report* 17 (September 2001): 1–16.

21. For the sometimes uneasy balance of professional schools within universities, see Derek Bok, *Higher Learning* (Cambridge, Mass.: Harvard University Press, 1986).

22. See Richard J. Cox, "Drawing Sea Serpents: The Publishing Wars on Personal Computing and the Information Age." *First Monday* 3, no. 5 (May 1998), at www.firstmonday.dk/issues/issue2_8/cox/index.html.

23. See Richard J. Cox, "Accountability, Public Scholarship, and Library, Information, and Archival Science Educators," *Journal of Education for Library and Information Science* 41 (Spring 2000): 94–105.

24. Stephen Jay Gould, *The Lying Stones of Marrakech: Penultimate Reflections in Natural History* (New York: Harmony Books, 2000), 223.

25. Jane Fritsch and David Rohde, "Trade Center's Past in a Sad Paper Trail," *New York Times*, September 14, 2001, at www.nytimes.com/2001/09/14/nyregion/14PAPE.html (accessed September 15, 2001).

26. Roberta Witty and Donna Scott, "Commentary: Firms Need Recovery Plans," CNET News, September 13, 2001, at news.cnet.com/news/0-1003-201-7149701-0.html?tag=lh (accessed September 15, 2001).

27. See, for example, L. Murphy Smith, "Planning for Disaster," *CPA Journal Online* (June 1994), at www.nysscpa.org/cpajournal/old/16097614.htm (accessed September 13, 2001).

28. Jeff Bailey, "Iron Mountain Is at the Peak of Records-Storage Industry," *Wall Street Journal*, September 18, 2001, at interactive.wsj.com/archive/retrieve.cgi?id=SB1000778212678095520.djm&template=pasted-2001-09-18.tmpl (accessed September 24, 2001).

29. Joseph Menn, "Paper Documents Destroyed but Electronic Records Survive," *LA Times*, September 12, 2001, at www.latimes.com/news/nationworld/nation/la-091201info.story (accessed September 12, 2001.)

30. Jonathan D. Glater, "Corporate Paper Trails Lie Buried in Soot," *New York Times*, September 13, 2001, at www.nytimes.com/2001/09/13/business/13LAWY.html (accessed September 13, 2001).

31. For example, James R. Chiles, *Inviting Disaster: Lessons from the Edge of Technology* (New York: HarperBusiness, 2001) considers fatal "system fractures" resulting from human error and mechanical problems, and Edward Tenner, *Why Things Bite Back: Technology and the Revenge of Unintended Consequences* (New York: Alfred A. Knopf, 1996) examines how technological solutions often create more problems than those trying to be solved, ranging from medicine to other supposed technological innovations.

32. The statement was posted on the Archives and Archivists Listserv, September 14, 2001 14:29:19 –0400.

33. I have made a preliminary effort to reflect on this in my "Records Programs, Disaster Preparedness, and Recovery: A New Urgency," *Records and Information Management Report* 17 (January 2002): 1–14. This is included, in a revised form, as the third chapter of this book.

34. Greg Cresci and Arindam Nag, "Key Data Lost in Terror Attack but Seen Regained," Reuters, September 12, 2001, at biz.yahoo.com/rf/010912/n12279148_2.html (accessed September 15, 2001).

35. Shannon McCaffrey, "Legal Industry Suffers Major Blow," Associated Press, September 15, 2001, at dailynews.yahoo.com/h/ap/20010915/us/attacks_lawyers_4.html (accessed September 18, 2001).

36. John Seely Brown and Paul Duguid, *The Social Life of Information* (Boston: Harvard Business School Press, 2000). For an earlier article incorporated into this book see John Seely Brown and Paul Duguid, "The Social Life of Documents," *First Monday* 1 (May 1996), at www.firstmonday.dk/issues/issue1/documents/index.html. For a related article, see David M. Levy, "The Universe is Expanding: Reflections on the Social (and Cosmic) Significance of Documents in a Digital Age," *ASIS Bulletin* 25 (May/June 1999), at www.asis.org/Bulletin/Apr-99/the_universe_is_expanding___.html.

37. Discussions about knowledge management are legion, but a continuing useful orientation to it is Thomas H. Davenport, *Information Ecology: Mastering the Information and Knowledge Environment* (New York: Oxford University Press, 1997).

38. Quoted in Lisa Singhania, "Financial Firms Put It Together," *USA Today*, September 12, 2001, at www.usatoday.com/money/finance/2001-09-12-rebuilding.htm (accessed September 13, 2001).

39. Quoted in Joan D. LaGuardia, "Investors Fear a Paperwork Nightmare," *News-Press*, September 13, 2001, at www.news-press.com/biz/today/010913records.html (accessed September 15, 2001).

40. Steve Vogel, "Tear-Stained Spreadsheets: Army Office That Lost Half Its Staff Reconstructs a Year's Work," *Washington Post,* October 10, 2001, B1, at www.washingtonpost.com/wp-dyn/articles/A33788-2001Oct9.html (accessed October 11, 2001).

41. For an assessment of these programs, refer to Richard J. Cox, Elizabeth Yakel, David Wallace, Jeannette Bastian, and Jennifer Marshall, "Archival Education in North American Library and Information Science Schools," *Library Quarterly* 71 (April 2001): 141–194 and "Educating Archivists in Library and Information Science Schools," *Journal of Education for Library and Information Science* 42 (Summer 2001): 228–240.

42. Jesus Sanchez, "Destruction Leaves Firms Searching for Quarters," *LA Times*, September 12, 2001, at www.latimes.com/la-091201real.story?coll=la-home-utilities (accessed September 13, 2001).

43. Terence Riley, "What to Build: Two Architects, an Urban Planner, a Structural Engineer, and a Landscape Designer Consider the Future of Ground Zero," *New York Times Magazine*, November 11, 2001, 92–94, 96.

44. Peter Behr, "Wall Street Firms Struggle to Cope With Staff Losses," *Washington Post*, September 13, 2001, E01, at www.washingtonpost.com/wp-dyn/articles/A21153-2001Sep12.html (accessed September 18, 2001).

45. Eli M. Noam, "Terror Tests the Fabric of the Communication Network," *New York Times*, September 17, 2001, at www.nytimes.com/2001/09/17/technology/17NECO.html?ex=1001744134&ei=1&en=a8a10a60f2d66415 (accessed September 18, 2001).

46. For example, William J. Mitchell, *City of Bits: Space, Place, and the Infobahn* (Cambridge, Mass.: MIT Press, 1995) and *e-topia: "Urban Life, Jim—but Not As We Know It"* (Cambridge, Mass.: MIT Press, 2000). In the earlier book Mitchell examines how computer networks are redesigning the city, just as earlier railroads, automobiles, telephones, and new commercial networks transformed urban life. The more recent book examines whether cyberspace has killed the city, concluding cyberspace's influence may be no greater than earlier developments such as postal systems, electrification, and the automobile.

47. A prime example remains Sherry Turkle, *Life on the Screen: Identity in the Age of the Internet* (New York: Simon and Schuster, 1995), but other disciplines have chimed in, such as C. A. Bowers, *Let Them Eat Data: How Computers Affect Education, Cultural Diversity, and the Prospects of Ecological Sustainability* (Athens: University of Georgia Press, 2000) and Barry Sanders, *A Is for Ox: Violence, Electronic Media, and the Silencing of the Written Word* (New York: Pantheon Books, 1994).

48. Simon Romero, "Attacks Expose Telephone's Soft Underbelly," *New York Times*, October 15, 2001, at www.nytimes.com/2001/10/15/technology/15PHON.html?ex=1004149942&ei=1&en=9209ae6c8e9fc523 (accessed October 16, 2001).

49. *New York Times*, September 21, 2001, B13.

50. *New York Times*, September 13, 2001, A2; September 26, 2001, A20; October 3, 2001, A19.

51. See "Teaching Students about Terrorism and Related Resources," at askeric.org/Virtual/Qa/archives/Subjects/Social_Studies/Current_Events/tragedy.html. [This website has since changed to askeric.org/cgi-bin/printresponses.cgi/Virtual/Qa/archives/Counseling/tragedy.html.]

52. Bill Carter and Felicity Barringer, "At U.S. Request, Networks Agree to Edit Future bin Laden Tapes," *New York Times*, October 11, 2001.

53. Check Daniel Dayan and Elihu Katz, *Media Events: The Live Broadcasting of History* (Cambridge, Mass.: Harvard University Press, 1992) or Johanna Neuman, *Lights, Camera, War: Is Media Technology Driving International Politics?* (New York: St. Martin's Press, 1996), among the hundreds of media studies. How are these being used in information science schools?

54. For a wide array of writings on these topics, see Philip E. Agre and Marc Rotenberg, eds., *Technology and Privacy: The New Landscape* (Cambridge, Mass.: MIT Press, 1997); David Brin, *The Transparent Society: Will Technology Force Us to Choose between Privacy and Freedom?* (Reading, Mass.: Addison-Wesley, 1998); Amitai Etzioni, *The Limits of Privacy* (New York:

Basic Books, 1999); Angus MacKenzie, *Secrets: The CIA's War at Home* (Berkeley: University of California Press, 1997); David M. Rabban, *Free Speech in Its Forgotten Years* (Cambridge: Cambridge University Press, 1997); Natalie Robins, *Alien Ink: The FBI's War on Freedom of Expression* (New Brunswick, N.J.: Rutgers University Press, 1992); Jeffrey Rosen, *The Unwanted Gaze: The Destruction of Privacy in America* (New York: Random House, 2000); H. Jeff Smith, *Managing Privacy: Information Technology and Corporate America* (Chapel Hill: University of North Carolina Press, 1994) and Janna Malamud Smith, *Private Matters: In Defense of the Personal Life* (Reading, Mass.: Addison-Wesley, 1997).

55. Murray Sayle, "Hijacking Television," *Prospect* (October 2001), at www. prospect-magazine.co.uk/highlights/hijacking_oct01/index.html (accessed September 29, 2001).

56. Sayle, "Hijacking Television."

57. Stanley Kurtz, "Free Speech and an Orthodoxy of Dissent," *Chronicle of Higher Education*, October 26, 2001, B24.

58. Patrick Thibodeau, "Information Security Will be Key with Lawmakers," September 17, 2001, at www.cnn.com/2001/TECH/industry/09/17/information.security.idg/index.html (accessed September 20, 2001).

59. Philip Shenon, "Ashcroft Wants Quick Action on Broader Wiretapping Plan," *New York Times*, September 18, 2001, at www.nytimes.com/2001/09/18/national/18CONG.html?todaysheadlines (accessed September 18, 2001).

60. Carl S. Kaplan, "Concern Over Proposed Changes in Internet Surveillance," *New York Times*, September 21, 2001.

61. Kevin Poulsen, "Hackers Face Life Imprisonment Under Anti-terrorism Act," *Business Week*, September 25, 2001, at www.businessweek.com/technology/content/sep2001/tc20010925_5807.htm (accessed September 29, 2001).

62. William Glaberson, "Technology's Role to Grow in a New World of Security," *New York Times*, September 18, 2001, at www.nytimes.com/2001/09/18/ national/18RULE.html?todaysheadlines (accessed September 18, 2001).

63. Alan Travis, "Identity Cards: Un-British or Vital? The ID Debate," *The Guardian*, September 25, 2001, at politics.guardian.co.uk/attacks/story/0,1320,557630,00.html (accessed September 29, 2001).

64. Bruce Craig, *NCC Washington Update* 7, no. 39 (September 27, 2001).

65. Bruce Craig, *NCC Washington Update* 7, no. 43 (October 18, 2001).

66. See "The Post-September 11 Environment: Access to Government Information," at www.ombwatch.org/article/articleview/213/1/1/.

67. Ron Southwick, "Colleges Largely Complying with Requests for Information on Foreign Students, Survey Finds," *Chronicle of Higher Education*, October 4, 2001, at chronicle.com/free/2001/10/2001100403n.htm (accessed October 5, 2001).

68. Jim Puzzanghera, "FBI Pursuing Clues to Terrorists on Internet and in E-Mail: Forensic Teams Searching Computer Files in Florida Public Libraries Where Suspects May Have Left Tracks," *Mercury News*, September 19, 2001, at www0.mercurycenter.com/local/center/internet0920.htm (accessed September 24, 2001).

69. Katie Hafner, "In the Next Chapter, Is Technology an Ally?" *New York Times*, September 27, 2001, at www.nytimes.com/2001/09/27/technology/circuits/27TECH.html?ex=1002598492&ei=1&en=bcaa7b1d0aeea9ac (accessed September 29, 2001).

70. See this issue of his newsletter at www.counterpane.com/cryptogram-0109a.html.

71. "Tech Sector, Already Weak, Disrupted by Attacks," *New York Times*, September 20, 2001, at www.nytimes.com/reuters/technology/tech-attack-technology.html?ex=1002093116&ei=1&en=9040d8a7247e05cf (accessed September 24, 2001).

72. See, for example, Carl Shapiro and Hal Varian, *Information Rules: A Strategic Guide to the Information Economy* (Cambridge, Mass.: Harvard Business School, 1998).

73. See, for example, Thomas K. Landauer, *The Trouble with Computers: Usefulness, Usability, and Productivity* (Cambridge, Mass.: MIT Press, 1995).

74. Stewart Brand, *The Clock of the Long Now: Time and Responsibility* (New York: Basic Books, 1999), 88.

75. Whether such a site of tragedy should be memorialized is an issue that Americans, and others, have wrestled with before; see Kenneth E. Foote, *Shadowed Ground: America's Landscapes of Violence and Tragedy* (Austin: University of Texas Press, 1997).

76. Raymond LaFever to the Archives and Archivists Listserv, September 13, 2001 11:59:49 –0400. Within days a group of archives—including the New York State Archives and the National Archives Northeast Region (serving as co-coordinators); the Archivists Roundtable of Metropolitan New York; New York University's Program in Archival Management and Historical Editing; Columbia University; New-York Historical Society; the New York City Department of Records and Information Services; the American Records Management Association-New York City; and the METRO Library Agency—had joined together to work on disaster assessment and recovery and to document the World Trade Center destruction. Additional information about these efforts can be found at a website established by the State Archives at: www.nyshrab.org/WTC/wtc.html.

77. "Documentary Records First of NYC Air Attacks" September 17, 2001, at www.cnn.com/2001/SHOWBIZ/News/09/17/attack.film.reut/index.html (accessed September 19, 2001).

78. Neal Gabler, "This Time, the Scene Was Real," *New York Times*, September 16, 2001, at www.nytimes.com/2001/09/16/weekinreview/16GABL.

html?rd=hcmcp?p=03wKM03wS243sgO012000mQRnYQRgk (accessed September 19, 2001); Elvis Mitchell, "Good at Action Films. Maybe Too Good," *New York Times*, September 18, 2001, at www.nytimes.com/2001/09/18/movies/18NOTE.html?rd=hcmcp?p=03wKK03wS243sgO012000mQRnYQR gk (accessed September 19, 2001).

79. Angus Kress Gillespie, *Twin Towers: The Life of New York City's World Trade Center* (New Brunswick, N.J.: Rutgers University Press, 1999).

80. Richard W. Wiggins, "The Effects of September 11 on the Leading Search Engine," *First Monday* 7, no. 10 (October 2001), at firstmonday.org/issues/issue6_10/wiggins/index.html. See also the Pew Internet Report on Internet use after September 11 at www.pewinternet.org/reports/toc.asp? I Report=46. Among other things the report concluded, "Perhaps the most significant development online after the attack has been the outpouring of grief, prayerful communication, information dissemination through email, and political commentary. Nearly three-quarters of Internet users (72%) have used email in some way related to the events to display their patriotism, contact family and friends to discuss events, reconnect with long-lost friends, discuss the fate of the victims, and share news."

81. Eugene S. Schweig, Joan Gomberg, Paul Bodin, Gary Patterson, and Scott Davis, "The Internet: Shaking up Scientific Communication; How a Regional Mailing List Facilitated Response to an International Event," *Nature*, July 26, 2001, at www.nature.com/nature/webmatters/equake/index.html.

82. Stephen Schwartz, "The 'Ladenese Epistle': What You Can Learn from Reading Osama's Oeuvre," *Weekly Standard* 7, no. 7 (October, 2001), at www.weeklystandard.com/FreePDF/FreePDFPopup.asp.

83. Brewster Kahle to archivists@yahoogroups.com, Archives and Archivists Listserv, September 16, 2001 07:48:59 –0700.

84. Andrea Foster, "2 Scholars Archive Web Sites on Terrorist Attacks," *Chronicle of Higher Education*, September 18, 2001, at chronicle.com/free/2001/09/2001091801t.htm (accessed September 19, 2001).

85. Leslie Walker, "Web-Page Collection Preserves the Online Response to Horror," *Washington Post*, September 27, 2001, E01.

86. Bruce Craig, "Cultural Institutions Impacted by World Trade Tower Disaster," *NCC Washington Update* 7, no. 38 (September 20, 2001).

87. Information about the library at the Pentagon can be found at www.hqda.army.mil/library/.

88. BFanning to the Archives and Archivists Listserv, October 1, 2001 14:59:22 –0400.

89. For a popular account, see Brand, *The Clock of the Long Now*.

90. As we were working on this document, several students from the Middle East have withdrawn and gone back home. With 173 international students out of our total 865 students, restrictions or individuals merely declining to

come here because of concerns about safety can have a serious impact on the school (and, indeed, the entire university). We have also received inquiries about transferring to our program from other schools in the New York and D.C. areas, so it is possible that there may also be some new students coming to the school.

91. See, for example, Jeff Opdyke, "Your Money Matters: Do You Know Where Your Vital Records Are?" *Wall Street Journal*, October 10, 2001, at www.nj.com/newsflash/index.ssf?/cgi-free/getstory_ssf.cgi? f0118_BC_WSJ—YourMoneyMatters&&news&newsflash-financial (accessed October 11, 2001).

92. Similar questions have been asked before, such as by Francis Miksa, "The Cultural Legacy of the 'Modern Library' for the Future," *Journal of Education for Library and Information Science* 37 (Spring 1996): 100–119.

93. See Julie Thompson Klein, *Interdisciplinarity: History, Theory, and Practice* (Detroit, Mich.: Wayne State University Press, 1990).

94. Eric Ormsby, "The Battle of the Book: The Research Library Today," *The New Criterion* (October 2001): 7.

95. Richard J. Cox, "Debating the Future of the Book," *American Libraries* 28 (February 1997): 52–55.

96. The classic study on this is Marion Paris, *Library School Closings: Four Case Studies* (Metuchen, N.J.: Scarecrow Press, 1988).

97. James J. O'Donnell, *Avatars of the Word: From Papyrus to Cyberspace* (Cambridge, Mass.: Harvard University Press, 1998), 90, 156.

CHAPTER THREE: PREPARING

INTRODUCTION

We never had seen anything like it. Two 110-story aluminum-clad towers hit by airplanes, burning, and then collapsing into twisted piles of rubble. The loss of human lives was tragic. And within hours the World Trade Center destruction was also a records issue unlike any we had witnessed in the United States.

As we watched our television screens we saw paper documents floating around lower Manhattan. "It was one of the most dramatic images from the World Trade Center attack: a confettilike blizzard of paper floating to the ground amid the fiery devastation," writes one group of reporters.[1] Another report begins, "A crumpled page of cleaning instructions with a reminder to damp-wipe smudges and smears. A blank check from a financial firm on the 101st floor. A tattered résumé, shreds of a faxed message, a cell-phone bill, a note about school, a bank statement, an expense report. A request for a promotion dated 1979. Personal and official, all shapes and sizes, bits of paper blanket Lower Manhattan with the mundane poetry of office life. They drifted from the sky on Tuesday and fell to earth miles away in Brooklyn, sheets and scraps that document the 28-year life and abrupt death of the World Trade Center."[2]

Another article describes an attorney searching for the files of a divorce case he was engaged in, and the reporters muse, "Computer technology was supposed to have prevented this. And to a large degree, it did. Computers saved reams of business data, which were backed up routinely in whirling databases miles from lower Manhattan. Yet it has become painfully clear here that the paperless life remains a fantasy. The loss of mere paper—and the ephemeral information scrawled, stamped or typed on it—has created an unexpected chaos that ranges from the serious to the trivial."[3] Chaos, confusion, and disorder all seemed to be the prevailing notions of what was occurring as the World Trade Center lay in heaps and the Pentagon sat wounded and ablaze.

Then we began to tick off the names of companies occupying the towers or residing nearby—Bank of America, Morgan Stanley, American Express, Lehman Brothers Holdings, and Merrill Lynch—and the long-term financial ramifications of record and information recovery became obvious. We also learned that many government agencies also were severely damaged in the attack, including the Securities and Exchange Commission, the Equal Employment Opportunity Commission, the Secret Service, and the Internal Revenue Service.

Added to this was the fact that many of these companies and government agencies lost not just records but large portions of their staff. Organizations relying on electronic information systems had most of their records and information backed up sufficiently (especially since many had already survived the 1993 terrorist attack on the World Trade Center), but none anticipated the scale of human loss. Individuals who would have played key roles in the recovery of records and information systems were gone. Suddenly, in horrific terms, the relationship of knowledge management to records and archives administration was clearer than ever. You could save all the records and information systems, but their usefulness depended on the people who created, maintained, and used them. Generally, in disaster planning, no one anticipated such an immense loss of people, usually focusing on the recovery of collections (libraries, archives, and museums) or information systems (businesses and government) and assuming that staff with critical knowledge would be available for assistance.

Just as mind-boggling was the percentage of Manhattan's office space that was destroyed, with estimates going into the millions of square feet. Once we could move past the patriotic reactions to the rebuilding of these twin towers, it was possible to understand that we might not need to or want to build such structures with the immense concentration of resources and people. The predictions being made for years regarding networked, virtual organizations suddenly seemed both more relevant and necessary. In one tragic event the kinds of virtual cities projected by visionaries like William J. Mitchell seemed to be not just a futuristic fantasy but a strategic objective.[4] We had seen this before. A century ago the Progressive reformers pushed the City Beautiful movement, aiming for the first large-scale urban planning incorporating wider streets, more parks, and an enhanced aesthetic sense offered by monuments and coordinated architectural design; the only cities able to pursue such aims were those, like Baltimore and San Francisco, that suffered large-scale destruction by fires or earthquakes, opening up wide areas for rehabilitation.

Records professionals did begin to discuss how to respond to this disaster, but, initially at least, the responses reflected more about the differences between archivists and records managers than about how we should approach such events. Archivists began ruminating about how to document the World Trade Center destruction. Records managers began considering how to cope with the loss of paper and electronic records they could see graphically portrayed on their television sets. Despite the differences in approaches that such discussions revealed about the various segments of the records professions (nothing we did not already know), the terrorist attacks of September 11 revealed that records and information management would get more attention (both as organizational and societal resources and as evidence in tracking down those responsible for the attacks) and the disaster preparedness and recovery business (already grossing billions of dollars) would continue to grow.

In the aftermath of these events, it seems useful to revisit some basic matters regarding disaster preparedness and recovery. It has been a decade since a standard records-management technical-report series (the original place for publishing this chapter) featured descriptions of how to prepare for and react to disasters, whatever their source or magnitude. A basic discussion of disaster planning was provided,[5] along with a reconsideration of the notion of vital records,[6] the notion of risk management and insurance,[7] and actions designed to deal with the disaster recovery of electronic records and information systems.[8] All of these previous publications continue to provide sound advice. The magnitude of recent events along with their political and international dimensions should make us want to reconsider just what we (archivists and records managers, as well as related professionals like librarians) mean by disaster planning and recovery.

AN EMERGING DISCIPLINE OR FOCUS?

Archivists, records managers, and librarians have been concerned with disaster preparedness and planning for many decades. Years ago, this concern was mostly connected to the concept of vital records (records designated as being essential for the ongoing work of organizations).

After identifying these records, we stored them in safe places, microfilmed them, and, later, backed them up in order to ensure that should our facilities be destroyed or heavily damaged, the critical documents would be available for reconstituting orderly operations.

Even before this, many records programs (the focus of the chapter here, although certainly libraries and librarians can relate what is happening here with their own situations) emerged with the assistance of or in the climate of civil defense or war contingencies. The origins of many government-records-management programs date to the late 1940s and 1950s when concern about the increasingly tense Cold War translated into concern for protecting the infrastructure of our government and society.

Now many terms float about that relate to this function: emergency preparedness, crisis management, incident response, disaster preparedness and recovery, continuity planning, business resumption, and e-continuity. One observer notes that in the last decade the "tenets of disaster recovery and business resumption" have been "broadened to embrace important concepts from each of those disciplines." Writing before the September 11 events, this individual attributes these changes to the "increasingly distributed technology, highly integrated applications and systems, and greater dependence upon complex electronic relationships" and the "federal government's urgent concerns over cyber-terrorism, information warfare" with its mixing of "information security/mission continuity requirements . . . without concern for boundaries between the disciplines."[9] Clearly, the pace of change affecting this functional responsibility has increased substantially in the past few months.

Some also have described a disaster planning and recovery "culture." Norm Harris lamented a few years ago that because of the emphasis on trying to build support from the top management down within an organization that individuals responsible for disaster recovery have neglected "middle management, lower management, supervisors, and individual staff members."[10] With the new emphasis on everyone being alert for changes or strange indicators in their surroundings, this no longer should be an issue. Harris argues that creating this culture means involving "as many staff and organization levels as possible in a risk assessment and risk identification"; conducting a "detailed security review"; holding meetings about disaster preparedness; developing a "business impact analysis"; distributing ideas about "disaster recovery ideas to different levels of management within the organization"; and creating a "policy state-ment and objectives for top management's approval."[11] The events of September 11 may have created a permanent or long-lasting foun-dation for this climate. No one will probably have to work very hard anymore to capture people's attention about potential disasters.

When individuals in the records and library worlds began trying to get people's attention about the possibilities of disasters a few decades ago, it was harder to accomplish this. The focus then was on natural disasters, mostly. We worried about fire, storms, floods, and earthquakes. There would be a severe storm, a flood, and records would become moldy or be threatened with total loss. A fire would sweep through a building, charring records and disrupting com-puter networks. We might then reflect on man-made disasters such as hazardous-materials accidents and other accidents. The growing reliance on electronic information networks increased the possibili-ties for mishaps, and we moved to consider events such as building failures, technological disasters like viruses, and even criminal ac-tivities whereby systems were deliberately sabotaged or looted. Now, we have to include terrorism and war, and with this both the possibilities and range of possible problems grow exponentially. It is one thing to prepare against the accidental; it is altogether more dif-ficult to have to be ever vigilant against the increased anticipation of a disastrous event.

A basic primer on disaster planning commences in this way: "Nat-ural disasters, such as Hurricane Andrew's August 1992 assault on southern Florida and Louisiana, make all of us acutely aware of our vulnerabilities to disaster. Fortunately, catastrophes of this magni-tude are rare, but disaster can strike in many ways. For example, a broken water main inundated the Chicago Historical Society in 1986; fire severely damaged the Cabildo in New Orleans in 1988; the Loma Prieta earthquake damaged several San Francisco area museums and libraries in 1989; smoke from an electrical fire covered collections throughout the Huntington Gallery in 1985; mold damage threat-ened Mount Vernon's archival collections. Large or small, natural or man-made, emergencies put an institution's staff and collections in danger."[12] While written from the perspective of libraries or archival repositories, the important matter here is both the description of the nature of the events and the frequency of the events. We may be in an era when major disasters can no longer be thought of as rare events but must be considered likely or even probable incidents.

TERRORISM: A NEW KIND OF DISASTER

Terrorism seems to change the rules of disaster planning and even recovery. People are told to try to learn about the nature of terrorism, something that was not usually done in terms of other kinds of disasters, and the kinds of targets terrorists select. We did not need to understand a flood or a fire (at least extensively) in order to respond to the results of their occurrences; our focus normally would be on the peculiarities of the materials and systems we were responsible for maintaining. We move quickly, then, from the accidental to the deliberate act. We prepare by learning about the kinds of weapons used by terrorists, and then we are advised to be alert to our surroundings, the people nearby, where and when we travel, and a long litany of other kinds of advice that differ to varying degrees from what we have normally thought of when we engaged in exercises about disaster planning and recovery. Being more focused on biological weapons and chemical threats during such an emergency is very different than simply being aware of potential hazardous materials. The idea is that you are under attack, not just endangered.

There are many aspects of dealing with terrorism threats that are covered in becoming prepared for more traditional catastrophes. Mostly what alertness for terrorism brings to the mix is a heightened sense of being aware of potential problems, and making sure that the organization is well connected to continuing news and reports about potential problems. Advice about terrorism from the Federal Emergency Management Agency (FEMA) starts: "Learn about the nature of terrorism." It continues: "Terrorists look for visible targets where they can avoid detection before or after an attack such as international airports, large cities, major international events, resorts, and high-profile landmarks. Learn about the different types of terrorist weapons including explosives, kidnappings, hijackings, arson, and shootings. Prepare to deal with a terrorist incident by adapting many of the same techniques used to prepare for other crises."[13] Here we see an obvious shift in disaster preparedness from response to awareness. As we have learned in the September 11 events, the potential utter destruction that a terrorist attack can inflict makes disaster preparedness both more urgent and somehow different in its focus.

The range of threats is broadened, of course, to include challenges like bomb threats, but an organization that is already well prepared for dealing with other natural and man-made disasters should be able to make the transition to dangers posed by terrorism more easily than those who have not worked on disaster planning and recovery. Fortunately the depth of experience and availability of guides, technical reports, and case studies can provide a place for any organization to begin to prepare itself for coping with worst-case scenarios.

The September 11 attacks on the World Trade Center and the Pentagon will help organizations to learn more about how to cope with the threat of terrorism. While the Federal Emergency Management Agency has long had a basic fact sheet on terrorism (available at http://www.fema.gov/library/terrorf.htm), reports of the aftermath of the September 11 events suggest new lessons that we have not been as well prepared for, such as significant trauma and stress that grows substantially after the immediate incidents and the lack of preparation for the loss of recovery-team staff leading to problems in coping with the impact of the disasters.[14] This suggests that terrorism means a new critical need for a greater depth of preparation if organizations expect to resume their operations. We need to review our approaches to disaster planning and recovery in light of these new possibilities of destruction.

A REVIEW OF THE ELEMENTS OF DISASTER MANAGEMENT AND PREPAREDNESS

Most experts in disaster planning and management suggest that there are four critical aspects related to this function: prevention, preparedness, response, and recovery. Prevention relates to the "activities involved in reducing the probability of a disaster and reducing the probability of loss should a disaster occur," encompassing a records-management program, vital-records operation, and business continuity planning. Preparedness includes "planning activities to assist the organization in responding to an emergency event if one does occur," involving a disaster plan, training staff, stockpiling emergency supplies, and using recovery vendors. Response "includes the activities involved in activating the plan and assembling resources when a disaster occurs," ranging from "contacting relevant authorities and response and recovery team members," "contacting recovery resources and vendors," "conducting an initial assessment of damage," "securing affected areas," and "activating contingency arrangements." The recovery phase "includes the activities required to restore records and operations so that normal business can resume," encompassing "stabilizing the environment," "conducting a full assessment of damage to records," "removing and treating damaged records according to established priorities and procedures," "repairing damaged facilities and returning records to their appropriate location," and "evaluating response and recovery activities and updating plans."[15]

Nearly every manual, article, or technical report on disaster planning and recovery emphasizes the necessity of a written plan. Here is typical and good advice for what such a plan should include: "Remember three important characteristics of an effective disaster plan: comprehensiveness, simplicity, and flexibility. The plan needs to address all types of emergencies and disasters that your institution is likely to face. It should include plans for both immediate response and long-term salvage and recovery efforts. The plan should also acknowledge that normal services may be disrupted. How will you proceed if there is no electrical power, no water, and no telephone?" Particularly important is the accessibility of the plan: "The plan must be easy to follow. People faced with a disaster often have trouble thinking clearly, so concise instructions and training are critical to the success of the plan. The key is to write in a clear, simple style without sacrificing comprehensiveness. Above all, remember that you cannot anticipate every detail, so be sure that while your plan provides basic instructions, it also allows for some on-the-spot creativity."[16]

Writing these plans has become a seemingly straightforward process, whereby the elements of a plan are fairly standard, including statements about authority and decision making, the kinds of events covered by the plan, actions to be taken, various procedures and persons involved, instructions about how to restore normal activities, and explicit information about emergency services and resources, contact information, checklists of steps to be taken, and other forms guiding disaster responses. But it is important that what seems like a fairly formulaic process not become one that is taken for granted. The events of September 11 may prove helpful to all organizations in the long run as these organizations shake off their complacency and revisit disaster planning and recovery. If an institution has had such a plan in effect for many years without any mishaps it is indeed fortunate. However, it may also be the case that these plans have become outdated or, worse, invisible and not known by employees who will be needing them should something catastrophic occur.

The matters of planning and writing clear advice in a plan that can be followed in the event of a disaster have become more complex in these days of terrorist attacks, but such advice is still important. Organizations must shift through their mandates, activities, and various responsibilities in order to enhance the possibility of an appropriate and effective response to threats or actual destruction. The difference may be, as the World Trade Center destruction suggests, that the extent of destruction or damage assumed to be handled in the previous disaster preparedness efforts is far out of proportion from what we might face in the future. More recently, what we term disaster planning has been placed within a broader process of "risk analysis." One author, for example, provides a series of related definitions related to risk analysis, including risk analysis itself involving "identifying the most probable threats to an organization and analyzing the related vulnerabilities of the organization to these threats"; "risk assessment" with a focus on "evaluating existing physical and environmental security and controls, and assessing their adequacy relative to the potential threats of the organization"; and a "business impact analysis" encompassing "identifying the critical business functions within the organization and determining the impact of not performing the business function beyond the maximum acceptable outage."[17] Add the recent level of international terrorism to the mix, and somehow risk analysis or disaster planning seems to be in need of reconceptualization.

Such ideas suggest, of course, that disaster planning and preparedness is an ongoing function, requiring leadership, resources, and organizational commitment. When such planning began to be advocated and carried out in the 1970s, first among libraries and then museums and archives, it was common to witness a flurry of training for the process and the preparation of plans that then sat unused. I once saw the only copy of a disaster plan sitting on top of a file cabinet in the middle of the main office complex; obviously, the plan would be among the first items that would be destroyed if a disaster occurred. The new sense of disaster preparedness that has developed through recent years because of the increasing use of and reliance on information networks and the threats of terrorist activity makes such a soft commitment to disaster preparedness very weak (as it actually always has been). We have known for a long time that a disaster plan is important, but now we must understand that it is essential.

THE PLAN

Key to being prepared to cope with a disaster is a written plan. Such plans provide detailed instructions about disaster preparedness, what to do if a disaster occurs, and the actions necessary after the disaster happens. Most experts contend that it is essential that an organization assemble a team of people to prepare the plan, and in this way disaster planning is like any other organizational strategic planning. Indeed, advice on disaster planning from Australia has an organization starting the process by considering the following: the "functions of the agency and how they impact on stakeholders"; the "regulatory and operational framework"; the "agency's goals and objectives and strengths and weaknesses"; and the "agency's role in relation to National, State and Local bodies responsible for disaster management."[18] This is essentially the same beginning point for any planning effort.

Some identify five phases in developing a disaster plan, including conducting a risk analysis; identifying already present preventive and preparedness procedures; recommending additional preventive and preparedness procedures; allocating responsibilities; and developing procedures to respond to and recover from disasters. All such planning efforts have been put in place to minimize the risks of a disaster occurring. In this new era of international terrorism, however, the focus might need to be both on trying to lessen the occurrence of a disaster and on the preparation of dealing with the disaster when it occurs. While we can plan for natural disasters such as storms and floods (especially since we can know if we are in a region where we are susceptible to severe weather), the nature of terrorism is to be unexpected.

The degree to which we can be prepared for dealing with such events also will vary greatly according to the nature of the organization we work for. Disaster preparedness plans always have had to be formulated with an eye towards certain kinds of limitations, such as the availability of funds, the nature of the facilities, and the availability of staff trained to work with records and who are knowledgeable about how to respond to disasters. There will be obvious gaps between the nonprofit cultural institution and the for-profit large corporation and the ability to rectify these variables and to be able to respond to disasters in this new era. All of these organizations are, however, at the same point of needing new training about terrorism and being more reliant on the government's ability to warn and to protect us from future attacks.

One might also expect that there would be differences in planning and preparation between organizations that are involved in industries tied to national defense, security, and other strategic activities that would enhance their prominence as potential targets and cultural organizations such as archives, libraries, and museums. We have learned, however, that cultural organizations are just as often targeted for destruction because of their symbolic value and national identities. The World Trade Center appears to have been a target not just because of its role in the global economic system criticized by Islamic fundamentalists but because of its symbolic role for American and Western capitalism. Everyone needs to ask what might make their organization a potential target, and then take the necessary actions intended to protect their facilities, holdings, and staff.

To have a sense of how things have changed in the aftermath of the terrorist attacks in the United States, we can examine how generally we have considered the matter of the successful implementation of these plans. "One of the best methods of maintaining staff awareness is to practice the plan regularly," notes one expert who then playfully suggests, "One way of practicing the plan, which is not recommended, is to have frequent disasters. Indeed, if the plan is effective, frequent disasters should be prevented. However, in some instances, such as in very old buildings and in tropical countries frequent disasters are often unavoidable. Regardless of the frequency of unavoidable disasters, training sessions, including mock disasters, should be held on a regular basis to ensure that all staff are familiar with the disaster plan."[19] While practice is certainly advisable, the nature of the avoidance of the disaster has changed. In the United States we have assumed that such disasters would be infrequent and when they did occur that they would be the result of more normal natural disasters or the occasional human error. Now we must practice in order to prepare for a completely different kind of event. Now we must practice as if a disaster will occur.

There are many templates available for use in compiling a disaster plan. Here is a standard one for libraries and archives offered by a regional conservation center, suggesting the body of the plan include the following:

- **Emergency information sheet:** one-page summary of immediate steps to be taken and individuals to be contacted.
- **Introduction to the plan:** its purpose, author, organization, scheduled updates.
- **Communication plan (or "telephone tree"):** names of those to be contacted, including office and home numbers, strategy for contacting them, and communication vehicles that can be used.
- **Institution-wide collection priorities:** list, with locations and name/phone of collection specialist(s). *Note:* More detailed priorities—by department, subject, and/or location—should be indicated in an appendix to the plan.
- **Prevention/protection strategy:** schedules, procedures, and persons responsible for routine testing and inspections (e.g., of fire alarms and suppression systems, roof, etc.), and procedures for follow-up to reported vulnerabilities. *Note:* Inspection checklists should appear in the appendix, and completed inspection forms should be retained to allow follow-up on reported problems.
- **Checklist of pre-disaster actions:** outline of procedures to be followed in advance of emergency for which there is advance warning (e.g., hurricane, flooding), including assignment of responsibilities for those actions.
- **Instructions for response and recovery:** summary of steps to be taken to salvage materials. It is useful in the body of the plan to summarize the procedures for the most likely incidents, and to include both more detail and a broader range of incidents in the appendix.

It is then suggested that there be a number of appendices, including ones with information on

- **Recovery team members:** list of recovery/salvage team members (including work and home phone numbers), with description of their responsibilities, scope of authority, and reporting lines.

- **Collection priorities within departments, locations, and/or subject areas:** lists, names of collection specialist(s) for each area, and location (perhaps indicated on floor plan).
- **Checklists for prevention/protection inspections:** extra copies of forms to be used.
- **Response and recovery instructions:** detailed, step-by-step instructions on all phases of salvage operation, including discussion of recovery from the range of incidents that are possible (e.g., roof/plumbing leaks, flooding, fire, etc.) and covering the various media included in the collection, such as books and journals, manuscripts/records, coated vs. uncoated stock, sound recordings, photographic media, computer/electronic media, etc.
- **Instructions for long-term rehabilitation:** procedures for activities including marking and labeling, rebinding and repair, rehousing manuscript/archival materials, sorting and rehousing, smoke/soot removal, cleaning, etc.
- **Record-keeping forms:** multiple copies of all forms that may be needed in the salvage operation, including inventory forms, packing lists, requisitions and purchase orders, etc.
- **Detailed building plans:** separate sets covering each of the following: storage areas, aisles, entrances and exits, windows; fire extinguishers, fire alarms, sprinklers, smoke/fire detectors, annunciators; shut-offs and master switches for power, water, gas, HVAC (heating, ventilation, and air-conditioning) system, elevator controls, etc.; priority collections (by department).
- **Resource lists:** locations and inventory of in-house supplies, sources of commercial supplies/equipment that may be purchased, names of consultants and other specialists, sources of auxiliary/volunteer personnel, etc. For lists of resources outside the institution, it will be useful to provide day and night/weekend contacts and phone numbers, along with some details about the resource such as the type and quantities of materials available, cost and payment terms, and/or special arrangements/contracts that exist.
- **Accounting information:** description of institutional funds available in a recovery effort and procedures/authorization for access to them.
- **Insurance information:** explanations of coverage, claim procedures, record-keeping requirements, restrictions on staff/volunteers entering a disaster area, information on state/federal disaster relief procedures.

- **Location of keys:** information about the location of, and means
  of access to keys or combinations for special collections, eleva-
  tors, offices, etc. *Note:* For security reasons, it may not be pru-
  dent to provide exact information about all these. In such cases,
  the plan should specify a procedure for contacting the individuals who have the proprietary information.
- **Reading list:** location and call number of materials in the collection, and perhaps full text of key works.[20]

While this template would need to be updated to encompass the
business organization and to take into account the need to deal with
information technology networks and some of the different challenges posed by the threat of terrorist activities, the basic elements
remain useful guides for other organizations needing to develop
such plans.

NEW THINKING

Not too many years ago when organizations approached disaster
planning and preparedness they could follow reasonably simple
guidelines for building awareness, developing plans, and identifying resources and expertise. The emergence of networked organizations and the occurrence of terrorist attacks have created a need for
a new kind of approach. Before the events of September 11, expert
Robert Campbell wrote, "Quite simply, as disruption tolerances
shrink to hours, minutes and nanoseconds, the business continuity
planner must move into areas of computer viruses, unauthorized access, denial-of-service attacks, and other hostile actions where potential abuse and misuse can seriously disrupt critical operations."[21]
It is true that much of the earlier disaster planning and responsive-
ness advice had been built on a somewhat more leisurely approach
dealing with traditional (largely paper-based) library, archives, and
museum materials. Electronic information systems add new dimensions to the business of disaster planning and recovery.

We also need a new kind of thinking when it comes to how we
measure success or failure in disaster planning and recovery. One
expert notes, regarding the success of these efforts, "the main reason
for failure is lack of awareness: plans do not work if they remain on
a shelf. People make plans work, by being familiar with their con-

tents."[22] In the realm of terrorism, however, success is dependent on an entire government and nation's ability to be prepared. "People" becomes not just organizations but nations and governments, the media, and a network of advisers, experts, and other sources. It is much more complex than planning a response to a flood or fire, even taking into consideration that there are many unforeseen and constantly changing aspects of these kinds of disasters.

In other earlier approaches to disaster planning and recovery, we measured success by what we could save. The World Trade Center destruction is such absolute destruction, however, that recovery is now measured not by what is relocated and saved but by the ability of the organization to stay afloat. This has always been the focus of business disaster planning, especially as larger financial enterprises have shifted so much of their records and information into electronic systems that can be backed up and accessed from off-site. Disaster planning is really much more along the lines of risk assessment and contingency planning. When you see entire art, artifact, and archival collections wiped out in a matter of minutes with no hope of recovery, we have evolved into a very different kind of function.

Older measures for measuring success become antiquated. Consider these: "frequency of disasters; time required for the library to return to normal operations; quantity of material lost; value of material lost; quantity of material requiring conservation; time required to repair the building; response of staff to disaster; whether they can operate in less than optimal conditions and maintain reasonably high morale."[23] In the catastrophic destruction of a terrorist attack, like that we witnessed on September 11, most of these are hardly possibilities. At the least, they become lower priorities because of the need to try to recover human lives and to see to the welfare, physical and emotional, of the employees of organizations affected by such tragic occurrences.

Another different aspect is how we weigh human life and the costs of collections, archival holdings, and vital records. Even the older traditional approaches to disaster planning would state something like this: "The first priority in any disaster is human safety. Saving collections is never worth endangering the lives of staff or patrons. In a major event, the fire department, civil defense authorities, or other professionals may restrict access to the building until it can be fully evaluated. Once safety concerns are met, the next consideration will be records and equipment crucial to the operation of the institution, such as registrar's records, inventories, and administrative files. Collections salvage and building rehabilitation will be the next priority."[24] The large loss of human life during the September 11 terrorist attacks reveals that human life protection or the more grisly recovery of remains in such occurrences may transform the heart of disaster planning and recovery.

Should We Hire a Consultant?

Hiring a consultant to assist with a new effort or to revise or review an existing policy can never hurt an organization. There are many vendors providing disaster-planning services as well as individual consultants who can assist an organization work on disaster planning. The World Wide Web lists many companies offering such services, with many of them specializing in particular aspects of materials, paper or electronic, or kinds of disasters, fire or flood. One of the tasks that each organization will have to engage in is to locate, meet with, evaluate, and maintain contacts with commercial vendors specializing in such services or individuals who can provide consulting services. Ideally, locating such services and expertise in the immediate area so that they can be quickly called in for assistance is ideal.

It is important to proceed with caution in hiring a service vendor or employing a consultant. One technical leaflet on disaster management suggests, "It is important to note, however, that while consultants may be useful for assessing risks, preparing plans, and carrying out recovery operations, it takes time to develop a knowledge of organizations. The importance of having internal knowledge, secured by employee participation and training, cannot be underestimated."[30] This seems like excellent advice. It suggests, as well, the importance of an organization making an ongoing commitment to disaster preparedness. It also suggests the importance for larger organizations to have on staff an individual who is the resource person or coordinator for disaster planning and recovery, one who brings expertise through formal training and other experience as well as a sound knowledge of the nature of the organization and its activities, mandates, and priorities.

Peter Waters, considering how to work with water-damaged archives and library materials, argues that "it cannot be emphasized too much that no general instructions can take the place of an assessment of a given situation on site by a qualified, experienced li-

brary or archive specialist, who has proven experience in the reclamation of fire and water-damaged collections. It is strongly recommended that such assistance and advice be sought at the earliest moment after a disastrous event has occurred."[26] Obviously an
institution needs to do disaster preparedness work that enables it to
have its own knowledgeable staff, aware of their own facility and
holdings, ready to connect with individuals and service agencies
particularly well versed in disaster-recovery situations.

The Differences between Paper and Electronic Records

There are differences in dealing with damage to paper materials
and electronic systems utilizing computers. Peter Waters describes
how "paper absorbs water at different rates depending on the age,
condition, and composition of the material. Thus, some understanding of the mechanism of swelling action, as well as the development
of mold, is essential to planning a successful salvage operation."[27]
The physical appearance of damaged books and manuscripts also
suggests the extent of water damage. Water-damaged paper materials also must be dealt with quickly, as mold can begin to emerge
within forty-eight hours. Weather becomes an important factor:
"Weather is often the critical factor in determining what course of
action to take after any flood or fire in which archive and library materials are damaged. When it is hot and humid, salvage must be ini-
tiated with a minimum of delay to prevent or control the growth of
mold. When the weather is cold, more time may be taken to plan
salvage operations and experiment with various reclamation procedures."[28] Cleaning, drying, freezing, and other procedures become
important steps to be taken in trying to recover paper materials
damaged by water.

Computers are susceptible to damage and disaster as well. The
most common threats, besides catastrophic events, are overheating
of computer rooms; water damage; increasing humidity; fire and
smoke; power supply spikes, drops, and other fluctuations; deliberate sabotage; and dust. The recovery of computer systems most
often focuses on repairing or replacing equipment and the retrieval
of backed-up data on the systems (and as the costs of equipment
fall, the data tends to be the primary concern). That dealing with
computer systems can be very different is evident when one vendor suggests that as problems arise they be recorded in a "history

log" and that system users, site managers, security personnel, maintenance individuals, service bureaus, and individuals at re- mote locations all be notified. Furthermore, computer system prob- lems are usually measured by financial parameters: "In a survey commissioned by INTRA COMPUTER, Inc., it was revealed that 16% of those responding reported a system-stopping 'incident' caused by environmental conditions at least six times annually, and that for 12% of respondents the minimum estimated dollar cost of each incident was over $50,000. It is clear, from these statis- tics, that for companies meeting the respondent's profile with an annual risk exceeding $300K, the cost of Disaster Prevention can be instantly justified."[29]

The differences between the recovery of computer systems and traditional paper objects like paper records or artifacts and art ob- jects suggest the need for organizations to have identified the range and extent of their needs for assistance. This also suggests that for many organizations it will be difficult for one individual to possess the range of knowledge and skills needed to deal with all aspects of a disaster-recovery operation. This suggests that organizations will need to make sure that a staff person assumes a clearinghouse type of function, identifying the range of needs and those individuals and vendors that can provide services. It also strengthens the need for organizations to engage in planning involving the entire institu- tion so that everyone is invested in the process, all the priority records and information systems with value to the organization's survival are identified and provided for, and all internal expertise useful for disaster planning and recovery is identified.

The Differences between Cultural and Other Organizations

While there are many similar steps for preparing for disasters that *all* organizations should take, there are also some differences between cultural organizations with archival holdings and other institutions with archival and records-management programs. A business will be vitally concerned for estimating its potential fiscal loss, including such aspects as "increased operating costs," "loss of business opportuni- ties," "loss of financial management capability," "loss of assets," "neg- ative media coverage," "loss of stockholder confidence," "loss of goodwill," "loss of income," "loss of competitive edge," and "legal ac- tions."[30] Obviously, cultural agencies like archives, libraries, and museums have fiscal concerns as well (they are concerned, for example, about adequate insurance), but the focus of their disaster-recovery activities is not merely to restart operations but to recover their holdings and collections.

Another area of similarity is the increasing concern about security. In the 1970s libraries and archives became more interested in security because of the occurrence of well-publicized thefts from rare-books and archival collections. The exploits of thieves like Stanley Blumberg (rare books and manuscripts) and Gilbert Bland Jr. (rare maps) represent another, albeit seemingly benign, form of terrorism against libraries, archives, museums, and other cultural organizations.[31] These institutions were victims often because they were vulnerable to theft, at least before they had to adjust to a tightening up of security and access practices that has changed the environment in which scholarly research took place and which often attracted individuals to become scholars in the first place.

This sea change of attitudes and incidents led to workshops, new security devices and policies, manuals, and the cross-fertilization of ideas between security experts and cultural custodians. More recently, in business and government organizations, the growing reliance on electronic information networks and the use of the World Wide Web led to the phenomenon of hackers and concerns about breaches into proprietary databases with all sorts of privacy, rights, legal, and marketing issues; thieves like Blumberg and Bland also utilized the Internet to size up and identify potential libraries, archives, and museums as likely targets for their antics. Just a decade ago a study of a group of major financial institutions revealed how lackadaisical they had been about privacy.[32] The past decade of increasing news coverage about gaffs in the protection of personal privacy and the revelations about how terrorist and criminal groups often use these electronic networks has changed such perspectives. Experts on risk assessment note that now "security is an increasing concern because computer systems are increasingly complex. Particular security concerns result from the proliferation of PCs, local area networking, and online systems that allow more access to the mainframe and departmental computers. Modern technology provides computer thieves with powerful new electronic safecracking tools. Computer internal controls are especially important because computer processing can circumvent traditional security and control techniques."[33]

BONUSES (SILVER LININGS AND CLOUDS AND ALL THAT)

It might be possible, when reflecting upon the tragic events of September 11, to nearly give up and forget about disaster planning and recovery. The enormity of the destruction seems to make planning and almost any degree of preparedness an irrelevant exercise. Of course, organizations with backed-up electronic records and information systems were able to recover, hindered mostly by the loss of many staff. Even for organizations that seemed to lose everything, staff and records, a systematic approach to disaster planning brings other benefits. Listing geographic and climatic hazards will make the organization more aware of its surroundings and able to contend with disasters on a lower scale. Examining the building and site, even if it might ultimately be destroyed completely, can help the organization provide more secure housing for its records and other valuable data. Fire protection and electrical systems, plumbing, and environmental systems need to be regularly inspected and that inspection will bring with it a better facility. Looking at fire extinguishers, fire alarms, and a fire-suppression system has obvious ongoing benefits.

Doing disaster planning and recovery also helps an organization to gain greater sensitivity to the nature of their records and information systems. A traditional archives, library, or museum might become involved in such planning as a way "to determine the vulnerability of the objects within the collections. What types of materials are included? Are they easily damaged? Are they particularly susceptible to certain types of damage such as moisture, fire, breakage, and the like? How and where are collections stored? Are they protected by boxes or other enclosures? Is shelving anchored to structural elements of the building? Is it stable? Are any artifacts stored directly on the floor where they could be damaged by leaks or flooding?"[34] Obviously the questions and concerns will be different for an organization possessing much greater reliance on information technology or operating within a more intense for-profit competitive environment. Even these organizations may have art and other cultural resources as office decorations or even representing investments of the company that require a very different kind of preparedness than what the organization normally provides for its other operational assets. Again, we see here the increasing complexity and need for diverse expertise that has moved disaster planning and preparedness from routine function to a higher-end priority.

There is also the enhancement of cooperative thinking and acting. One guide states, "Disaster planning should not take place in a vacuum. To work effectively, it must be integrated into the routine operating procedures of the institution."[35] This may be far too limited a view. Engaging in a disaster-planning process connects the organization to other organizations, governmental agencies, and experts. There will be other benefits from such work. It will make the organization think through media relations, commercial suppliers and service providers, and local sources of potential help. And the process will make the organization reflect on all the other possible connections, institutional and individual. An added benefit may be that the process helps to bring together archivists, records managers, knowledge managers, and others in an effort with a very specific objective that helps everyone to see common points and similarities.

Engaging in disaster planning and recovery also provides an opportunity for organizational records programs to work with others and to gain a greater organization-wide profile. "It is important to include employees at all levels who represent functions of organization, and training should be given commensurate with the duties assigned," notes one reference on disaster management. "A typical mix of positions for a disaster management project for records would include: the Chief Information Officer or Corporate Records Manager, a computer analyst, the Occupational Health and Safety Director and the Building Manager."[36] Such a mix creates the opportunity for explaining why records are important for the organization, not just vital records for ongoing administration but archival records for organizational memory and so forth. Many knowledge managers often exclude or put on a lower level records managers and archivists; disaster planning provides an opportunity for them to gain a mutual appreciation of their attitudes, assets, and activities within a particular organization.

Given that disaster preparedness is supposed to be concerned with protecting the assets (in our case records and information systems or archives holdings) of an organization, many involved in gaining support for such programs wonder why it has been so difficult to gain what they believe is adequate support. "Top management, in reality, does only two things: they say 'yes' . . . or . . . they say 'no.' Everything else associated with their responsibilities leads up to and prepares them for these decision-making responses. Because these executives have given their support by providing for

these capabilities, their negative responses must, therefore, be the result of our inability to provide them with the information they require. It could be our failure to meet their expectations in a manner
required to convince them to say 'yes.'"[37] All of this may have
changed because of the September 11 events. Now organizations
that might have approached disaster preparedness cautiously might
be seeking to implement it. It will be up to records professionals to
develop new approaches that will gain support lasting beyond the
immediate crisis and danger. Some proponents of disaster planning
suggest that we must "create the disaster recovery culture within the
entire organization. In this environment, everyone accepts the responsibility that his or her job is important to the protection of the
organization's assets, and disaster recovery awareness is felt and
practiced by every staff member."[38] The events of September 11 have
certainly gotten everyone's attention about such issues, and we
must capitalize on this new awareness to build sensitivity to protecting assets like information and records systems.

ADDITIONAL BASIC READINGS

Fortunately, there are many basic and specialized references that can
assist in disaster planning. Basic references of particular usefulness
include Constance Brooks, *Preservation Planning Program Guides:
Disaster Preparedness* (Washington, D.C.: Association of Research Libraries, 1993); Judith Fortson, *Disaster Planning and Recovery: A How-
To-Do-It Manual for Librarians and Archivists* (New York: Neal-Schu-
man Publishers, 1992); Miriam B. Kahn, *Disaster Response and
Planning for Libraries* (Chicago: American Library Association, 1998);
V. A. Jones and K. E. Keyes, *Emergency Management for Records and
Information Programs* (Prairie Village, Kans.: ARMA International,
1997); and International Council on Archives, Committee on Disas-
ter Prevention, *Guidelines on Disaster Prevention and Control in
Archives* (Paris: ICA, 1997), all providing reasonably up-to-date in-
formation or at least the framework for disaster planning and re-
covery that can be supplemented through newer sources on the
World Wide Web. A broader work on disaster management is
Richard T. Sylves and William L. Waugh, *Disaster Management in the
U.S. and Canada*, 2d ed. (Springfield, Ill.: Charles C. Thomas, 1996).

There are some older, classic primers that remain extremely useful, if for no other reason than that they influenced subsequent re-

ports and manuals. These include Sally A. Buchanan, *Disaster Planning, Preparedness, and Recovery for Libraries and Archives: A Ramp Study with Guidelines* (Paris: General Information Program and UNISIST, United Nations Educational, Scientific, and Cultural Organization, 1988) and Mildred O'Connell, "Disaster Planning: Writing and Implementing Plans for Collections-Holding Institutions," *Technology and Conservation* (Summer 1983): 18–24. A good bibliography with references to many older manuals and case studies is Susan E. Schur, "Disaster Prevention, Response, and Recovery: A Selected Bibliography," *Technology and Conservation* (Summer 1994): 21–23; (Fall 1995): 23–34.

We also have a great variety of specialized manuals on particular kinds of disasters or certain kinds of damaged materials. Examples include Valerie Dorge and Sharon L. Jones, *Building an Emergency Plan: A Guide for Museums and Other Cultural Institutions* (Los Angeles: Getty Conservation Institute, 1999); Miriam B. Kahn, *Disaster Response and Prevention for Computers and Data* (Columbus, Ohio: MBK Consulting, 1994); National Fire Protection Association, *NFPA 909: Protection of Cultural Resources* (Quincy, Mass.: NFPA, 1997); Debra Hess Norris, *Disaster Recovery: Salvaging Photograph Collections* (Philadelphia, Pa.: Conservation Center for Art and Historic Artifacts, 1998); *Primer on Disaster Preparedness, Management, and Response: Paper-Based Materials* (Washington, D.C.: Smithsonian Institution, National Archives and Records Administration, Library of Congress, and National Park Service, 1993); SOLINET, *New Strategies for Regional Disaster Mitigation and Response, Proceeding of a SOLINET Preservation Conference, April 28, 1999* (Atlanta, Ga.: Southeastern Library Network, Inc., 2000); and Michael Trinkley, *Hurricane! Surviving the Big One: A Primer for Libraries, Museums, and Archives* (Columbia, S.C.: Chicora Foundation, 1993).

There are specialized journals and World Wide Web sites providing a continuous supply of new information about disaster planning, such as *Disaster Recovery Journal*, published quarterly, and a variety of websites such as the Natural Hazards Observer website (Natural Hazards Center at the University of Colorado, Boulder), (www.colorado.edu/hazards); Disaster Mitigation Planning Assistance (disaster.lib.msu.edu/disaster/); Disaster Preparedness and Response (palimpsest.stanford.edu/bytopic/disasters); Federal Emergency Management Agency (www.fema.gov); Library of Congress Preservation Directorate (www.lcweb.loc.gov/preserv); National

Fire Protection Association (NFPA) (www.nfpa.org); and National Institute of Disaster Restoration (www.ascr.org/nidr.htm).

NOTES

1. Susan Chandler, Melissa Allison, and Rob Kaiser, "Recovery of Records Daunting, but Doable," *Chicago Tribune*, September 13, 2001, at www.chicagotribune.com/business/chi-0109130289sep13.story? coll=chi%2Dbusiness%2Dhed (accessed September 14, 2001).

2. Jane Fritsch and David Rohde, "Trade Center's Past in a Sad Paper Trail," *New York Times*, September, 14, 2001, at www.nytimes.com/2001/09/14/ nyregion/14PAPE.html (accessed September 15, 2001).

3. P. J. Huffstutter, "Towers of Missing Paperwork: Countless Letters, Records Lost in the World Trade Center Ruins Delay Divorces, Business Deals," *Los Angeles Times,* October 30, 2001, at www.latimes.com/news/ nationworld/nation/la-103001paper.story (accessed November 1, 2001).

4. William J. Mitchell, *City of Bits: Space, Place, and the Infobahn* (Cambridge, Mass.: MIT Press, 1995) and *e-topia: "Urban Life, Jim—but Not As We Know It."*(Cambridge, Mass.: MIT Press, 2000).

5. Alan M. Levitt and Karla H. Conford, "Contingency and Disaster Recovery Planning," *Records & Retrieval Report* 7 (September 1991): 1–16.

6. Susan Bulgawicz and Charles E. Nolan, "Protection of Vital Information Assets: An Interdisciplinary Approach," *Records & Retrieval Report* 7 (December 1991): 1–16.

7. Keith Ninesling, "Risk Management and insurance," *Records & Retrieval Report* 8 (March 1992): 1–16.

8. H. Wayne Gardner and Brett Balon, "Disaster Contingency Planning," *Records & Retrieval Report* 8 (September 1992): 1–16.

9. Robert P. Campbell, "Continuity Planning in the New Millennium: The Convergence of Disciplines," 2000, at www.disaster-resource.com/cgi-bin/ article_search.cgi?id='16'.

10. Norm Harris, "The Care and Feeding of the Disaster Recovery Culture," 1997, at www.disaster-resource.com/cgi-bin/article_search.cgi?id ='38'.

11. Harris, "The Care and Feeding of the Disaster Recovery Culture."

12. Beth Lindblom Patkus and Karen Motylewski, "Disaster Management," Northeast Document Conservation Center, at www.nedcc.org/plam3/ tleaf33.htm. Reprinted with permission from *Disaster Planning for Cultural Institutions*, by Beth Lindblom and Karen Motylewski, published originally as *Technical Leaflet #183* by the American Association for State and Local History, Nashville, Tenn., 1993.

13. Federal Emergency Management Agency, "Fact Sheet: Terrorism," January 10, 1998, at www.fema.gov/library/terrorf.htm.

14. Richard Corcoran, "Lessons Learned from 9/11," *Contingency Planning and Management Online*, October 22, 2001, at www.contingencyplanning.com/article_index.cfm?article=393 (accessed October 22, 2001).

15. State Records. New South Wales. *Guidance for Senior Management on Disaster Management for Records*, at www.records.nsw.gov.au/.

16. Patkus and Motylewski, "Disaster Management."

17. Geoffrey H. Wold and Robert F. Shriver, "Risk Analysis Techniques: The Risk Analysis Process Provides the Foundation for the Entire Recovery Planning Effort," *Disaster Recovery Journal* 7, no. 3 (1997), at www.drj.com /new2dr/w3_030.htm.

18. State Records. New South Wales. *Guidance for Senior Management on Disaster Management for Records*.

19. Jan Lyall, "Disaster Planning for Libraries and Archives: Understanding Essential Issues," in *Proceedings of the Pan-African Conference on the Preservation and Conservation of Library and Archival Materials, Nairobi, Kenya: June 21–25, 1993*, ISBN 90-70916-51-7, p. 103–112. The Hague, Netherlands: IFLA, 1995. At www.nla.gov. au/nla/staffpaper/lyall1.html.

20. SOLINET, *Contents of a Disaster Plan*, Preservation Services Leaflet, at palimpsest.stanford.edu/solinet/displan.htm.

21. Campbell, "Continuity Planning in the New Millennium."

22. Lyall, "Disaster Planning for Libraries and Archives."

23. Lyall, "Disaster Planning for Libraries and Archives."

24. Patkus and Motylewski, "Disaster Management."

25. State Records. New South Wales. *Guidance for Senior Management on Disaster Management for Records.*

26. Peter Waters, "Procedures for Salvage of Water Damaged Library Materials," July 1993, at palimpsest.stanford.edu/bytopic/disasters/primer/ waters.html.

27. Waters, "Procedures for Salvage of Water Damaged Library Materials."

28. Waters, "Procedures for Salvage of Water Damaged Library Materials."

29. IntraComputer, Inc. "Automated Disaster Prevention in the Computer Room: From a Vendor, Some General Advice," at www.intracomp. com/contents.html.

30. Wold and Shriver, "Risk Analysis Techniques."

31. Nicholas A. Basbanes, *A Gentle Madness: Bibliophiles, Bibliomanes, and the Eternal Passion for Books* (New York: Henry Holt, 1995); Miles Harvey, *The Island of Lost Maps: A True Story of Cartographic Crime* (New York: Random House, 2000).

32. H. Jeff Smith, *Managing Privacy: Information Technology and Corporate America* (Chapel Hill: University of North Carolina Press, 1994).

33. Wold and Shriver, "Risk Analysis Techniques."

34. Patkus and Motylewski, "Disaster Management."

35. Patkus and Motylewski, "Disaster Management."

36. State Records. New South Wales. *Guidance for Senior Management on Disaster Management for Records.*

37. Harris, "The Care and Feeding of the Disaster Recovery Culture."

38. Harris, "The Care and Feeding of the Disaster Recovery Culture."

CHAPTER FOUR: TEACHING

INTRODUCTION

Library and information science (LIS) schools have had a long, but often unsteady, relationship with their university parents. In recent decades, some of these schools have been challenged as being irrelevant to the university and its mission, and some have even been closed. Many have responded by renaming themselves, adding undergraduate programs, using new instructional technologies to add distance-education programs, and building partnerships. Some of these initiatives have burdened their resources, while some have created tensions between the LIS schools and their traditional constituencies. Yet, these schools should be in the heart of the university's interest in the so-called Information Age, whether one believes that this era is unique or inflated by its own self-importance. One way in which LIS schools can demonstrate their effectiveness is by using their courses to focus their students on contemporary issues affecting the librarian, archivist, information scientist, or any other form of information professional.

Information technology exists in the world, influenced and affected by economics, culture, politics, and a variety of other factors. It is sometimes easy to forget this in a school of information sciences, except in those special courses (generally not required) intended to focus students on technology's contexts (such as a course on information ethics). Even in required courses intended to push students to look at the broader aspects of information and its technologies (at the University of Pittsburgh we have a required course entitled Understanding Information), many students become impatient with anything other than teaching the most basic how-to approaches.[1] Otherwise, the environment the student is introduced to mostly consists of technologies, techniques, methods, and skills, suggesting that all the students have to do is to master these attributes and go out and apply them in their employing institutions (and, indeed, sometimes employers suggest that this is all they want as well). The astute students, especially those who keep up with current events, will make the connection between hardware, software, and what we now call "wetware" (the human body), realizing that they have to understand the historical, social, cultural, organizational, and other aspects that affect how information and information technologies are viewed and used.

Occasionally an event of immense proportions reminds us of such relationships between technology, information, and humanity. The terrorist attacks of September 11, 2001 (hereafter referred to as 9/11), are the most recent (and perhaps most dramatic) example of such an event. Not only did this event mark another example of the widening gulf between the Middle East and the West, most poignantly demarcated by differing views on technology and progress, it displayed in its aftermath the pervasive influence, power, and limitations of information technologies. As such, 9/11 and reactions to it provide an excellent case study for present and future information professionals.

EDUCATION, INFORMATION SCIENCES, 9/11, AND ME

In a school of information sciences, stressing the education of individuals in archival, information, and library sciences, especially one with many international students, it seemed natural to use the events of 9/11 to enable students to understand more about technology, specifically information technology, and its role in the world, not merely as a set of tools but as both determining and reflecting factors in world events, geopolitical systems, and the global economy. Faculty in other schools quickly identified the relevancy of information and information technology in this new era of terrorism, such as in developing "tools and expertise to meet many of the information-related challenges," assisting the "government make better use of information and in shaping critical policy choices in sensitive areas such as access to information," and helping libraries understand their role as "sources of information for the public"—recognizing that this is a war reliant on information and its management.[2] Information professionals in the field also recognized that their world had changed, such as in the expansion of the roles of the Chief Information Officer to include "risk analysis, disaster recovery planning, employee protection, public relations, and scenario planning."[3]

The possibility of teaching a doctoral seminar on 9/11 and its implications derived from several sources. The most obvious reason that this course happened was that I had been scheduled to teach a doctoral seminar during our school's spring term (January–April), and I had not yet settled on a topic. My various offerings of doctoral seminars shift about in topics in order to accommodate the particular needs of the doctoral students likely to take the seminar, and over the previous five years I had offered seminars focused on the origins of the archives and library professions in the Progressive Era (1880–1930); historical research methods and archives, library, and information sciences; and issues in higher education and the place of LIS education and schools in the modern university. Before the events of 9/11 provided another option, I was contemplating designing a doctoral seminar focused on American presidential libraries and their societal roles as museum, library, archive, and public monument—an interesting case study that could appeal to a wide range of research interests of our doctoral students and reflected one of my own areas of research.[4] Presidential libraries provide ample opportunities to consider matters running the gamut from privacy and access to ownership of public records and government information to concerns such as fiscal implications of information management and historical issues in the creation and use of records systems. The startling 9/11 events provided a similar opportunity, but one also forcing students to track unfolding revelations by government agencies, the media, and social commentators and pundits.

The 9/11 events also fit well into my own peculiar research interests and views about what students in an LIS school should be learning. In developing the archives and records-management specialization within my school, I had included an emphasis on the social and policy implications of administering records, developing a course called Archival Access and Advocacy exploring the various public policy implications of records. Indeed, the organizing principle of my teaching in archives and records management was that records were essential for purposes of evidence, accountability, and public and organizational memory. This emphasis distinguished our program, in that it was much broader, from other archives programs stressing the use of evidence for historical research or from records-management educational programs focusing on the importance of records for organizational functions. Such interests were also reflected in my own writings about public-policy issues, ranging from the importance of records for organizations and society to debates with novelist and essayist Nicholson Baker about his critiques of library and archives preservation.[5] In my teaching in the MLIS core curriculum in my school, through the Understanding Information course, I had also stressed a broad view whereby students would examine a wide range of "documents"[6] such as books and libraries, records and archives, the news media, movies, artifacts and museums, monuments and historic sites, landscape and place, architecture and buildings, maps, photographs, orality, advertisements, and the World Wide Web. One can surmise how many of these information documents played a prominent role in the 9/11 events.

Even with my interests and previous teaching, I did not immediately develop the notion of preparing a special course on 9/11 and its implications for the information professions. As I watched the television news coverage of the terrorist attacks, the swirling tons of office records around the remains of the World Trade Center made me reflect on the implications of the 9/11 events for my own discipline, archives and records management. Then I began to wonder about the disaster recovery of both electronic office information systems and paper records systems in the World Trade Center and the Pentagon. I started informal conversations with my faculty colleagues about how they were viewing the 9/11 events, and I soon discovered that we were all beginning to think along similar lines, even if our varying notions of the information fields led us to different conclusions. I led an effort of a number of our school's faculty to write a formal essay exploring the implications, and we published an essay in the e-journal *First Monday* on the topic (published here as chapter 2), identifying areas like disaster preparedness and recovery, knowledge management, workplace design and location, technology and the human dimension (such as the use of cell phones and the impact on children), ethics and citizens' rights, information security, information economics, memorials and documenting the 9/11 events, the role of the Internet in the 9/11 events, information preservation, and the potential impact on current and the creation of new kinds of positions in the information professions.[7]

While the exercise of writing the essay eventually provided a basis for the course I taught on the 9/11 events, the immediate aftermath of the essay brought three disappointments. I hoped that my faculty colleagues would contribute to a special volume of essays on the implications of 9/11, but their interest waned fairly quickly. It is hard to criticize them since most were busy with other projects when the terrorist attack occurred. One of my colleagues, José-Marie Griffiths, did draw on the *First Monday* essay as she advised some federal agencies in the aftermath of 9/11, but her use of the essay was a rarity. I wrote an essay about the impact of 9/11 on disaster preparedness in the records-management field, but that and this present essay might be the only result of scholarship on 9/11 among the faculty of my school (now chapter 3).[8] A bigger disappointment was the dashing of my hopes that faculty discussions about 9/11 could serve as a unifying point for the disparate elements (information science, library science, telecommunications, and archives and records management) of my school, but again there seemed to be little interest in using these discussions for this purpose. I even had to remind the committee preparing the annual strategic plan for the school that the *First Monday* essay had been done and related to some of the goals and objectives described in the plan. But the greatest disappointment was the nearly complete silence that greeted the *First Monday* essay in both the information professions and among the faculty of the school. The silence was deafening, and it made me wonder if it was not confirmation of the lack of direct involvement by faculty in both public scholarship and public policy (although I hear informally that the essay was used and considered in a favorable light).[9]

THE COURSE AND ITS OBJECTIVES

The course I developed and taught about the implications of the 9/11 events for the information professions was intended to help information professionals, especially those at the doctoral level with a research agenda in the field, to gain an appreciation of how information and information technologies fit into a societal context, not to seek an understanding of the changing nature of the Middle Eastern and Western worlds (a topic and objective best left to others).[10] The course was not intended to provide any vilification of or justification for either the United States or the Middle East, Western notions of democracy or Islamic fundamentalism, terrorism or the military response to terrorism—all issues which have divided American universities in the aftermath of 9/11.[11]

The purpose of my course—entitled "A New Meaning for 9/11: Libraries, Archives, and Information Technology in a Catastrophic

Era"— and indeed all my courses, was to challenge the student about his or her assumptions about their vocational aims, the role of the information professional in modern society, and the significance of information technology in society and its organizations. The focus of the course was the changing world, drawing on the theme of the issue of the *Economist* (September 15–21, 2001) appearing immediately after the disasters and featuring a dramatic photograph of the collapse of the World Trade Center with a banner headline reading, "The Day the World Changed." The lead article in that issue compares the attacks to the 1941 Japanese attack on Pearl Harbor, stating, "This week has changed America, and with it the world, once again."[12] The *Economist* perceptively notes that "counter-terrorism" depends on both the "pooling of information" and "international co-operation," and with this we have a glimpse of the possibilities of the first Information Age war.[13]

Such challenges are something that I do not think a school of library and information science always does very well, partly because it is a professional school often peopled by individuals seeking a credential to practice (although in our school the course fits into an existing curriculum related to information ethics and policy).[14] Reading about how other faculty approached the events of 9/11 revealed that others also seek the aim of challenging their students. A political scientist notes, for example, that "as an educator in political theory myself, it is part of my vocation to challenge all those loyalties with which students enter college."[15] We do not do this very often in a professional school, where our orientation too often seems to be to get students in and out as quickly as possible and to ensure that they get jobs. The burgeoning of undergraduate and distance-education programs also seems to have pushed these schools' focus on credentials, student head counts, and tuition revenues to new heights. Challenges often seem to be an obstacle to these activities, just as more theoretical approaches seems to be seen as nuisances by the students who desire only to know *how* to do something. One political scientist reminds us that theory comes from *theorein*, "to see," and that the ancient Greeks had *theoroi* who visited other cities, observed what was going on, and then came back to report about this: "To 'theorize' was to take part in a sacred journey, an encounter with the 'other' in which the theorist would attempt to comprehend, assess, compare, and then, in idiom in his own city, explain what had been seen to his fellow citizens. This encounter would inevitably raise questions about the customs or practices of the theorist's own city."[16] The events of 9/11 seemed to me to provide the opportunity to visit another "city" and to understand information science, technology, and the professions in a different way.

The university is not immune from the trials and tribulations of society. In times of national crisis, the tensions on the campus often mirror or even intensify the tensions in other parts of society. Some have already noted that criticisms about outspoken faculty and students who have not supported the American response to the 9/11 attacks mimic the kinds of censorship and tensions that prevailed on campuses in the First World War and during the Red Scare of the 1950s.[17] Offering a course on the 9/11 events implied some risks, therefore, especially in a school with a large number of international students. Still, the university campus was also one place for trying to understand the events of 9/11, a different exercise than the incessant coverage offered by television news and other media outlets, which generally appears to be more interested in grabbing viewers' attention and increasing its ratings. Courses, workshops, and special events appeared on nearly every American campus. At Brown University, a seminar on the Vietnam War was changed to allow an exercise between Vietnam and the present war on terrorism. As the instructors report, "Collectively, the students showed us and each other that behind the events of September 11 is a worldview incommensurable with our own and fundamentally at odds with many of the values we hold dear, and in so doing, they outlined the magnitude of the task at hand."[18] In a similar fashion, the course I designed was intended to prod students into looking at the broader implications of their chosen vocations in the modern information professions or as future faculty in schools preparing information scientists, librarians, and archivists.

DESIGNING THE SEMINAR: SOME CONTEXT

The seminar (along with the laboratory and lecture) has been one of the hallmarks of instruction and learning in the American university since its beginnings in the last quarter of the nineteenth century. The seminar was seen as the vehicle by which students, guided by an expert faculty member, could pursue research and master a particular area of knowledge, learn research methodologies, and develop professional relationships with other students and faculty that would assist them in their future careers. The distinguishing mark of the university has been research, and the seminar was a key means of supporting research.[19]

Mixed in with the growing pains of the modern American university has been the tension between vocational attitudes and learning. In 1930 Abraham Flexner lamented, "Persons who sacrifice broad and deep university experience in order to learn administrative tricks will in the long run find themselves intellectually and vocationally disadvantaged. From the standpoint of practical need, society requires of its leaders not so much specifically trained competence at the moment as the mastery of experience, and interest in problems, dexterity in finding one's way, disciplined capacity to put forth effort."[20] Indeed, some have wondered just what the role of the American university is in society, beyond research and learning (and athletics), in helping that society cope with serious, unresolved, and persistent ills, injustices, and other problems.[21] This challenge becomes more complicated when we ask it of a professional school such as the kind supporting the library and information science professions. Here there is more pressure on applied skills and marketable or vocational talents. One commentator on the difficult role of the university as a societal institution suggests that some faculty will focus on their "research and teaching as forms of participation, and their knowledge as something significant to share with the community," while others will stress their role as "researchers and teachers, their audience as a small number of students and professional peers, and their rewards as resulting from student evaluations of teaching or peer reviews of research by a small circle of intellectuals."[22] No matter what one thinks of such issues, most within the university at least recognize that the professional schools represent the clearest connection of the university to a relevant, practical role in society, although many critics question even if this is enough.[23]

Schools of library and information science have been especially vulnerable to the tensions within the university about practical or vocational knowledge, leading to a spate of closings and threats of closings, hurried efforts to change their names, and initiatives to create new programs, especially at the undergraduate level.[24] Yet, it is possible that recent events like that of September 11 are drawing universities to try to prepare their students for coping with real-world scenarios, whatever they call such education. Given the profound roles in and implications of the terrorist acts for the information sciences, what we might be seeing (and perhaps missing) is a chance for the remade library schools to assume a higher profile within the university. In my teaching in my own discipline of archival studies, I include a strong emphasis on issues like advocacy and leadership.[25]

Schools of library and information science have supported a remarkable array of courses. My doctoral seminar, despite its focus on a very recent event, is not an anomaly, but it is typical of the kinds of courses that have been offered, especially those related to matters of policy. A description of a course on information policy offered more than a decade ago suggests many similarities in content if not focus. This course, offered at the University of Arizona, considered such matters as privatization, computer security, intellectual freedom, the news media, telecommunications, privacy, scientific and technical information, information as a commodity, and copyright.[26] Nearly twenty years ago, Kathleen Heim noted the need for the redefinition of public service for library and information science faculty, but she also worried that the mechanism of information policy was a "catch-all term for a bewilderingly complex set of regulations, rules, and laws," arguing that these faculty members must develop research in collaboration with "decisionmakers."[27] Around the same time, Michael Buckland described efforts at his school to transcend the theoretical or conceptual in a policy course where students were required to develop solutions to real-world problems.[28] The 9/11 events seem to provide an opportunity for this.

THE SEMINAR DESIGN: NUTS AND BOLTS

I adopted a combination of a reading and a writing seminar for this course, trying to lead the students into wide reading of the professional, research, and other literature related to information technology and its place in society and requiring the students to write a lengthy essay exploring a topic of interest to them and related to the 9/11 events and the information professions. Students were expected to participate in weekly seminar discussions focused on an assigned reading and to prepare a lengthy research paper related to some aspect of information (broadly defined) and "catastrophic" events. The paper could focus on aspects related specifically to the events of September 11 and their aftermath, or it could focus on some other aspect of information management, information technology, and the information professions and catastrophic events such as war, terrorism, natural disasters, espionage, or some closely related topic with a connection to September 11.

Each week's class session consisted of discussion in the first half of the assigned reading (and any other readings the students might wish to discuss based on their own work). Each week's class had a list of "suggested additional readings" providing some related background readings that students might want to explore or that they might already be familiar with from previous courses, other degree programs, or personal interests. I reviewed the various readings and framed some general discussion questions to get class discussion started. Students were expected to be prepared for the class discussion by having read either the primary assigned text or some other volume from the list of additional readings or one that the student had selected (with my permission).

The class discussions framed questions, issues, and implications related to the roles of librarians, archivists, and information scientists and their organizations in dealing with events of tragedy, catastrophe, and warfare. The class discussions were not intended to resolve any of these issues or topics; rather they were intended to assist students to think through the implications of what it means to be an information professional in modern society. Despite the fact that this was a doctoral seminar, not all of the readings were research studies, although those readings falling into this category led to discussions about the methodologies used by the authors in their work. The course also considered the matter of the information professional, the academic, and the idea of "public" scholarship (publishing outside academic or scholarly journals in areas affecting public opinion and policy), a topic that was ideally suited given the emphasis on the 9/11 events and the continuing media coverage of their aftermath. Many of the readings are examples of public scholarship.[29]

The second half of each class consisted of discussions by the students of their work on a major paper related to some aspect of dealing with catastrophic events from the perspective of archivists, librarians, and information scientists. These papers could examine past catastrophic events and their impact on libraries, archives, and information systems or the role of these organizations and their professionals in these events. And the papers could examine a particular issue from a historical, technical, or some other perspective, ranging from preparation of analyses of research done about these events from a library, archival, or information viewpoint to original research (if appropriate materials were available) on a past event to a proposal for a research study addressing such matters. Students were given great latitude in picking a topic related to their own interests and career objectives.

DELIVERING THE COURSE

The course considered as many divergent aspects of the 9/11 events and their implication for the information professions as possible. After an introduction to the course, I made a brief presentation stressing an orientation to the nature of professions, how information technology operates within society, the context of library and information science schools, the various ways we could consider the information professions and the technology, and reviewing the course structure and objectives. During this first class session, I reviewed some of the media allusions to the idea of "the day the world changed" and asked if we really had a sufficient perspective for determining if 9/11 was a unique event (emphasizing that we were engaging in an exercise of examining current events, with all the limitations that this can bring). Students were also encouraged to try to use the many websites that were being created about 9/11 events, as additional information became available about the topics we were considering and as an illustration of what role the web itself was playing.[30]

The course commenced with a background discussion about the World Trade Center (WTC) and its destruction. We started with a reading of one of the recent histories of the World Trade Center, stressing the importance of the WTC as a symbol of America and power, with eerie allusions to the 1993 bombing and insights into the cultural history of the buildings and site, including the technological challenges and aspects of the massive buildings.[31] It proved to be an excellent way to start the course. We considered why anyone would want to destroy the WTC, the nature of terrorism, and how symbols are often primary targets for terrorists,[32] and we considered whether we should rebuild the WTC and, if we did, how information and other technologies developed in the three decades since its construction would change its appearance and functionality. This led to spirited discussion about the role information technology plays in the design and construction of office and government buildings.

Since there has been such an extensive literature devoted to the role of technology in modern society, and since the West and its use of technology seems to have been a cause of a considerable aspect of the animosity felt toward it, the nature of and perspectives about technology were the next topics considered in the doctoral seminar. The primary reading suggested was Arnold Pacey's *The Culture of Technology*, a classic assessment of the political, social, cultural, and economic aspects influencing the role of technology in society.[33] I discussed the recent emergence of the concept of "social informatics," the "interdisciplinary study of the design, uses and consequences of information technologies that takes into account their interaction with institutional and cultural contexts,"[34] as a means of suggesting how LIS education was addressing these kinds of issues. I also discussed the various meanings, or lack of meaning, of the modern notion of an Information Age and how some see every era as revolving around some notion of information.[35] We considered how different information professions and different segments of society view technology, especially noting how there are often dramatically conflicting attitudes about technology. It was important to have this discussion in order to set the scene for understanding the media coverage of and political and government response to the 9/11 events.

The next class discussion was on "Technology, Modern Warfare, and Libraries, Archives, and Information Systems." One of the aims here was to demonstrate how the origins and subsequent development of information science have been closely intertwined with government and warfare, such as is reflected by the evolution of ARPANET (originally conceived for government, science, and technology uses) into the Internet and World Wide Web. The primary reading assignment was Paul Edwards's excellent study, *Closed World*, detailing the links between Cold War military projects, the evolution of digital computers, and the origins of cybernetics, cognitive psychology, and artificial intelligence and the idea of a "closed world" casting every event as a contest between the United States and the Soviet Union.[36] Understanding this connection is a problem I have consistently found among the students at our school, especially those interested in public, school, and other traditional library venues. In the post-9/11 events, it is especially important to comprehend since the newly coined notion of "netwar"—"an emerging mode of conflict in which the protagonists . . . use network forms of organization, doctrine, strategy, and technology attuned to the information age"[37]—is now a crucial aspect of our modern era. As Walter Laquer reminds us, "The number of potential targets is almost endless and is bound to grow along with the growth of information systems."[38]

The role of technology is so critical that this remained the focus in the course for the next several weeks. We considered the economics of information, the implications of technology for the individual, and the continuing debate about the implications of increasing reliance on technology as a source for catastrophes. While there were many aspects of information economics I could have looked at, I decided to focus on one of the prevalent themes in schools educating future librarians, the debate about information "haves and have nots" in this era. This seemed to fit well into the tension with the Western world's affluence as a justification for terrorism, while enabling the students to consider this traditional theme in library and information schools.[39] The class session on technology and the individual was an effort to assist the students to consider the broad array of technologies delivering information to them and how these were affected by the 9/11 attacks, reminding them of the news images of smashed computers and swirling paper records, whining screeches of electronic devices with their service disrupted, the use of cell phones, and the struggle with reestablishing the New York Stock Exchange. We considered how the cell phone, considered to be an obnoxious and unsafe device by many commentators,[40] was transformed into a tool for providing a rare (perhaps unheard-of) glimpse into events that we would not normally have known much about.

I also discussed a number of the critical works that have appeared about technology's impact on the individual, but I focused mostly on David Gelernter's engaging and angry discourse in his *Drawing Life* depicting his reaction to being badly wounded by the Unabomber in 1993.[41] Gelernter's tome was especially relevant given many of the reactions to the 9/11 terrorist attacks, and it served as a good connection to considering the catastrophic potential of technological dependence. The notion of catastrophe was a particularly real issue for the consideration of the 9/11 events with the unexpected collapse and total destruction of the WTC. The persistent potential of imminent disaster, made very real through James Chiles's *Inviting Disaster*,[42] was another topic that many of these students often do not seem to consider given their dependence on all sorts of technological devices and gadgets. It provided another opportunity to aid students to

consider the unintended consequences of technology that they sometimes miss because they often come to such a school intent on learning everything they can about how to use information technologies.
We considered how the devices that they believe are saving them
time or making their lives and jobs more efficient may be bringing
other negative aspects that counterbalance the advantages.[43]

The next few weeks reached into the heart of some of the most critical matters concerning the connection between the 9/11 events and
the information professions. A session on media and information led
to a spirited discussion about what we were learning and *not* learning
about the aftermath of the 9/11 events. Playing on the many com-
mentaries about how the constant re-airing of the WTC attack and collapse seemed like a Hollywood movie, we explored the role that radio, television, and web news media play in such events. The airing
of *9/11* by CBS on March 10, 2002, in the middle of the course, provided an opportunity to explore the transformation of the French documentary filmmakers' work and the nature of the kinds of insights
provided by the use of media such as this. We discussed the formali-
ties, rituals, and ceremonies of these media and their implications for
how we gain understanding in this so-called information era.[44]

The role of the news media provided quite a contrast to the ways
in which government viewed access to information about such
events. To set the appropriate tone, I quoted from the Declaration of
Independence's list of "injuries and usurpations" including that "He
[the King of England] has called together legislative bodies at places
unusual, uncomfortable, and distant from the depository of their
public Records, for the sole purpose of fatiguing them into compliance with his measures" (as a means of reminding the students that
access to government information has been an issue for a very long
time).[45] After some consideration of the federal government's history in information dissemination, I led a class discussion about the
immediate impact of the 9/11 events on this traditional role, especially the threat of the USA Patriot Act and its amending of most of
the major and recent government information statutes. As some
commentators have noted, "The Bush administration is the most se-
cretive Washington has seen in years," and the 9/11 scenario only
seemed to provide an excuse for it to pursue such secrecy.[46]

Drawing on the Athan Theoharis book on government secrecy, I
tried to show that government secrecy was not a new issue but that
increased secrecy as a result of the 9/11 attacks might be the great-

est and most long-term consequence of terrorism in America.[47] Two weeks later, one of the course sessions followed up with discussion about "National Defense, Security, and Individual Privacy and Rights," essentially trying to get students to wrestle with the very real tensions between these concerns and the legitimate reasons for such matters that are not always easy to balance in our society. As one commentator states, "We have the capacity to turn the United States into a surveillance society the likes of which the world has never seen. We could also significantly reduce the chances of a successful terrorist action in the future—a quite separate pursuit. It looks like Bush and Ashcroft are using September 11 as an excuse to clamp down on civil liberties, not as a wake-up call for solving these hard problems."[48] Obviously, such a juxtaposition of concerns and issues makes for spirited discussion that gets to the heart of what information professionals must consider in their work.

A major emphasis of my course was in assisting students gain an appreciation for the role of the city in information technology and in the memorialization and memory of events as a form of information document. In other words, students were asked to consider the long-term historical perspective of the information professions, society, and the uses of information technology. We considered the city as symbol of society and as major clusters of information technology and professionals, including the role that information technology (especially telecommunications and networks) has played in making cities possible (providing a nice connection back to the discussion about the role of technology in the construction of skyscrapers like the WTC). William Mitchell's books on the city and cyberspace provided the foundation for much of this discussion, and his futuristic writings were especially stimulating as we discussed what should be done with the lower Manhattan area where the WTC complex was located.[49] This provided a nice transition to the issue of memorials as information and the intense discussion going on in the media about how to remember the 9/11 attacks and its victims. I asked the seminar students to consider the most moving or effective memorials they had seen, and we discussed the general nature of memorials, their societal function, their timing, and how they change as information sources over time. Discussions about some of the historical writings about memorials which demonstrate how they are embroiled in the issues of their day—such as Kirk Savage's observation that "to be erected, monuments usually had to mesh with the beliefs and aspirations of the majority, even when those were so deep-seated that they were unspoken. And once monuments were erected, they reshaped those beliefs and aspirations simply by giving them a concrete form in public space"[50]—provided precisely the background needed to consider the present debates (rebuilding the WTC, or building parks, memorials, or museums) about the WTC, the Pentagon, and Flight 93.[51]

The last major topic for the seminar (before presentations by the students about their own papers) was that of the role of the World Wide Web. Given the importance of the web and all the attention to it, as well as the university placement and topic of the course, it would be easy to justify this as a subject that should have been considered earlier in the course or that should have been given more time for discussion. However, given that the students were being directed to use the web as a resource all through the course, concluding with a discussion about the web worked well. To some extent, we actually had considered throughout the course the use and value of the web as both a source of information about the 9/11 events and as a mechanism used by the terrorists themselves, reflecting both unfolding events in the aftermath of the 9/11 and the vast range of opinions held about the web.

CONCLUSION: EVALUATING THE COURSE

It is difficult to assess how effective this course was, primarily because we were considering events that were transpiring before our very eyes. As the course was wrapping up, for example, a number of books were appearing that both brought together interesting sources that would have been helpful for the seminar students and also provided some interesting insights into how the publishing industry functions with dramatic recent events.[52] This problem was especially evident when during the last week of the course, Edward Yourdon's book on information technology and 9/11 appeared, considering issues like security, risk management, and other issues.[53] It was clear that I would have used this book as a required reading, and it is also obvious that another version of this course (something I am not intending to do, by the way) would have an array of additional interesting readings to draw upon.

The students certainly seemed to be engaged during the course. Some of this was caused by their divergent backgrounds and experiences. Of the three students taking the course for credit, there was one from the United States with an interest in public-library administration, another from Botswana with an interest in archives and records management, and the third was from Egypt with an interest in higher education and academic libraries. Two individuals audited the course, including a doctoral student from Korea with a research interest in archives and records management, and a nondegree student with an academic background in history and a career in financial advising. All brought enthusiasm, intelligence, and strong opinions to the weekly sessions, and all engaged in interesting paper topics that contributed to the class discussion. The paper topics included an analysis of how library and information science schools in the United States were (or were not) responding to the 9/11 events, a comparison of American public librarians' response to 9/11 with how they responded to World War II, and the different reactions of American archivists and records managers to 9/11. While none of the final papers were, in my opinion, publishable, they did contribute to the lively class sessions.

If I were designing the course today, there are some changes I would make from what I did in the spring 2002 term. I provided the students many options for reading every week on particular topics. A bit of hindsight suggests that this diluted the focus of the class discussions a bit, where I had hoped that it would have provided a wider glimpse into the existing literature relating to the information professions, technology, and society. The diversity of reading detracted somewhat from our ability to analyze the approach, orientation, and credibility of the writings. Also, when I originally planned to design and offer the course, I had considered having a series of guest speakers attend class. I abandoned this idea in favor of a more coherent course (as sometimes guests do nothing but send a course into a million tangential directions). While I believe the course was a stable, coherent educational process, I now think that a few guest speakers or researchers might have helped diversify the course.

The main weakness, then, was the need to be a bit more flexible about the course and its topic than I normally would want to do. However, in a sense this provided an opportunity for all, instructor and students alike, to try to cope with current events that seemed to be constantly shifting and changing course. In retrospect, this made the course even more a part of the real world and provided some opportunity for us to consider how courses are constructed, evaluated, and, if appropriate, revised.

NOTES

1. I teach this course from time to time. In my version, I provide the following set of objectives: Understanding Information provides an appreciation of the underlying issues, debates, and factors defining the nature of information and the implications of these matters for the information professions. Information is a good (or commodity or resource) filling personal, organizational, and societal needs. Information is also organized and made available through complex information-handling systems. Information also comes to individuals, organizations, and society through a variety of means. And, issues and problems arise from interrelationships between information and individuals, society, organizations and systems, information technology, and the information professions. This course is intended to provide students knowledge about the responsibilities held by the information professions, but mostly this course is intended to assist students to comprehend the complexities of information in modern society and how the various notions of information affect or should affect the work of any information professional. The course is also intended to provide a theoretical and historical basis for the basic MLIS curriculum by helping students explore what information has been seen to mean by different groups and in different epochs. Course objectives include defining the nature of information, providing historic background on the nature of information systems, orienting students to concepts of information systems, integrating views of the physical and virtual library and other information providers, orienting students to technology issues related to information systems, making students aware of professional issues, making students aware of human factors influencing information systems, providing an orientation to information services, and providing an awareness of social, economic, political, and other issues affecting information systems.

2. Bruce Dearstyne, "Fighting Terrorism with Information: Issues and Opportunities," *Information Outlook* 6 (March 2002): 32.

3. Leslie D. Ball, "CIO on Center Stage: 9/11 Changes Everything," *Information Systems Management* 19 (Spring 2002): 9.

4. See my "America's Pyramids: Presidents and Their Libraries," *Government Information Quarterly* 19 (2002): 45–75.

5. See, for example, my most recent books: *Closing an Era: Historical Perspectives on Modern Archives and Records Management* (Westport, Conn.: Greenwood Press, 2000); *Managing Records as Evidence and Information* (Westport, Conn.: Quorum Books, 2001); coeditor with David Wallace, *Archives and the*

Public Good: Accountability and Records in Modern Society (Westport, Conn.: Greenwood Press, 2002); and *Vandals in the Stacks? A Response to Nicholson Baker's Assault on Libraries* (Westport: Conn.: Greenwood Press, 2002).

6. The documents concept builds off of John Seely Brown and Paul Duguid, *The Social Life of Information* (Boston: Harvard Business School Press, 2000) and David M. Levy, *Scrolling Forward: Making Sense of Documents in the Digital Age* (New York: Arcade Publishing, 2001).

7. Richard J. Cox with Mary K. Biagini, Toni Carbo, Tony Debons, Ellen Detlefsen, José-Marie Griffiths, Don King, David Robins, Richard Thompson, Chris Tomer, and Martin Weiss, "The Day the World Changed: Implications for Archival, Library, and Information Science Education," *First Monday* 6 (December, 2001), at firstmonday.org/issues/issue6_12/cox/.

8. Richard J. Cox, "Records Programs, Disaster Preparedness, and Recovery: A New Urgency," *Records and Information Management Report* 17 (January 2002): 1–14.

9. See my "Accountability, Public Scholarship, and Library, Information, and Archival Science Educators," *Journal of Education for Library and Information Science* 41 (Spring 2000): 94–105 and "Public Scholarship and Records Professionals," *Records and Information Management Report* 18 (April 2002): 1–14.

10. For example, Bernard Lewis, *What Went Wrong? Western Impact and Middle Eastern Response* (New York: Oxford University Press, 2001) represents a text seeking to understand the widening gulf between these societies and cultures. While such works were mentioned in the course, and there was some discussion of the differences affecting attitudes toward technology and progress, the focus of the course described here was on understanding just how information technologies fit into the real world with an emphasis on providing some level of comprehending the implications for the information professions.

11. Donald Kagan, "Terrorism and the Intellectuals," *Intercollegiate Review* 37 (Spring 2002): 3-8 is an example of a critique of the tendency of many academics to try to justify the actions of terrorists, reputedly by understanding, while lamenting, the decline of the tradition of moral education.

12. "The Day the World Changed," *Economist*, September 15–21, 2001, 13.

13. "The Day the World Changed," 14.

14. In a way, my course could be seen as an extension or addition of the ethics focus in our school. As the architects of this ethics focus describe it, "In our increasingly complex, multicultural, and information-intensive society, many critical issues related to information access and use are misunderstood, inadequately considered, or even ignored. . . . In a growing number of instances, decisions concerning information access and use are placing information professionals in sensitive, and sometimes vulnerable, positions." Toni Carbo and Stephen Almagno, "Information Ethics: The Duty, Privilege, and Challenge of Educating Information Professionals," *Library Trends* 49 (Winter 2001): 511.

15. Patrick J. Deneen, "Patriotic Vision: At Home in a World Made Strange," *Intercollegiate Review* 37 (Spring 2002): 34.

16. Deneen, "Patriotic Vision," 34–35.

17. Kevin Boyle, "A National Crisis and the Role of the Academy," *Thought & Action: The NEA Higher Education Journal* (Winter 2001-2002): 9–16. Much has been written about the response of the academy to the recent events, much of it being very negative (for example, students might wish to read Jerry L. Martin and Anne D. Neal, *Defending Civilization: How Our Universities Are Failing America and What Can Be Done about It* [American Council of Trustees and Alumni, November 2001], at www.goacta.org/sReports/defciv.pdf). A more balanced resource about how universities are responding to the post-September 11 events can be found at the National Association of State Universities and Land-Grant Colleges/Association of American Universities website (www.aau.edu/resources/resources. html): "This website has a dual purpose: to enable research university officials to share information on the ways campuses are addressing the challenges of the post-September 11 environment, and to provide links to other materials and website addresses they may find useful."

18. James G. Blight and Janet M. Lang, "Obstacles to Empathy: Teaching About Vietnam and the War on Terrorism," *Chronicle of Higher Education*, March 29, 2002, B12.

19. Laurence R. Veysey, *The Emergence of the American University* (Chicago: University of Chicago Press, 1965), 153–158; Christopher J. Lucas, *American Higher Education: A History* (New York: St. Martin's Press, 1994), 170–176.

20. Quoted in John T. Wahlquist, "The Graduate School," in P. F. Valentine, ed., *The American College* (New York: Philosophical Library, 1949), 522–523.

21. John J. Neumaier, "Can Universities Help Us Deal with Social Crises?" *Humanist* 40 (March/April 1980): 18–25, 56.

22. Barry Checkoway, "Reinventing the Research University for Public Service," *Journal of Planning Literature* 11 (February 1997): 311.

23. Robert M. Rosenzweig, *The Political University: Policy, Politics, and Presidential Leadership in the American Research University* (Baltimore, Md.: Johns Hopkins University Press, 1998), especially chapter 7.

24. See, for example, Michael Lorenzen, "Education Schools and Library Schools: A Comparison of Their Perceptions by Academia," *Illinois Libraries* 82 (Summer 2000): 154–159.

25. See Richard J. Cox, "Advocacy in the Graduate Archives Curriculum: A North American Perspective," *Janus*, no. 1 (1997): 30–41 and "Leadership and Archival Education," in Bruce W. Dearstyne, ed., *Leadership and Administration of Successful Archival Programs* (Westport, Conn.: Greenwood, 2001), 1–17.

26. Gretchen Whitney, "Information Policy and the Educated Librarian," *Government Publications Review* 17, no. 3 (1990): 221–235.

27. Kathleen M. Heim, "Dimensions of Faculty Public Service: A Policy Science Approach to Questions of Information Provision," *Journal of Education for Library and Information Science* 26 (Winter 1986): 161.

28. Michael K. Buckland, "Undecidable Decisions: Education for Library and Information Policy Analysis," in Roy D. Tally and Ronald R. Deultgen, eds., *Information Choices and Policies: Proceedings of the ASIS Annual Meeting 1979* (White Plains, N.Y.: Knowledge Industry Publications, Inc., for the American Society for Information Science, 1979), 51–57.

29. For background reading, see my "Accountability, Public Scholarship, and Library, Information, and Archival Science Educators" and "Public Scholarship and Records Professionals," cited earlier.

30. For example, students were asked to look at the American Association of University Presses bibliography of "books from university and scholarly presses that shed light on some of the issues surrounding the terrible events of recent days." These publications include works on the World Trade Center; terrorism; grief, loss, and trauma; catastrophe and disaster management; war, peace, and global issues; the Middle East and Islamic States; fundamentalism and political Islam; Islamic thought and culture; and aviation and airport security. This site is located at www.aaupnet.org/news/spotlight.html. Other sites included one offered by the *New Yorker* with its coverage of the September 11 events and aftermath and an array of other related articles and reports from its archives, available at www.newyorker.com/FROM_THE_ARCHIVE/PREVIOUS/; the University of Chicago Press site, at www.press.uchicago.edu/News/daysafter.html, with a series of essays, "Reflections by our authors in the aftermath" and descriptions of books the press has published on Islam, global war and peace, and ethnic conflicts and violence; and the site of the Social Science Research Council, "After September 11th: Perspectives from the Social Sciences," a "collection of essays by leading social scientists from around the country and the world . . . intended as resources for teachers—especially college and university instructors—who want to address the unfolding events in their courses from the perspectives of the social sciences" (www.ssrc.org/sept11/).

31. Angus Kress Gillespie, *Twin Towers: The Life of New York City's World Trade Center* (New Brunswick, N.J.: Rutgers University Press, 1999).

32. At the time of the course I drew on two works for discussing terrorism: Walter Laqueur, *The New Terrorism: Fanaticism and the Arms of Mass Destruction* (New York: Oxford University Press, 1999) and Ahmed Rashid, *Taliban: Militant Islam, Oil, and Fundamentalism in Central Asia* (New Haven, Conn.: Yale University Press, 2000).

33. Arnold Pacey, *The Culture of Technology* (Cambridge, Mass.: MIT Press, 1983).

34. Rob Kling, "What is Social Informatics and Why Does it Matter?" *D-Lib Magazine* 5 (January 1999), at www.dlib.org/january99/kling/01kling.html.

35. For example, Michael E. Hobart and Zachary S. Schiffman, *Information Ages: Literacy, Numeracy, and the Computer Revolution* (Baltimore, Md.: Johns Hopkins University Press, 1998).

36. Paul N. Edwards, *The Closed World: Computers and the Politics of Discourse in Cold War America* (Cambridge, Mass.: MIT Press, 1996).

37. David Ronfeldt and John Arquilla, "Networks, Netwar, and the Fight for the Future," *First Monday* 6 (October 2001), at firstmonday.org/issues/issue6_10/ronfeldt/index.html. Or, examine the full text of their study, *Networks and Netwars: The Future of Terror, Crime, and Militancy*, at www.rand.org/publications/MR/MR1382/.

38. Laqueur, *The New Terrorism*, 76.

39. The primary reading assigned this week was Michael Perelman's *Class Warfare in the Information Age* (New York: St. Martin's Press, 1998), with its contention that the selling of information and the treatment of information as a commodity reduces access to information, but I also discussed, in order to reflect the very different views about this topic, Barry Sanders, *A Is for Ox: Violence, Electronic Media, and the Silencing of the Written Word* (New York: Pantheon Books, 1994); Jorge Reina Schement and Terry Curtis, *Tendencies and Tensions of the Information Age: The Production and Distribution of Information in the United States* (New Brunswick, N.J.: Transaction Publishers, 1995); and Herbert I. Schiller, *Information Inequality: The Deepening Social Crisis in America* (New York: Routledge, 1996).

40. See, for example, Sidney Callahan, "Turn off That Cell Phone! Bare Your Soul in Private," *Commonweal* 127 (June 16, 2000): 7–8.

41. David Gelernter, *Drawing Life: Surviving the Unabomber* (New York: Free Press, 1997).

42. James R. Chiles, *Inviting Disaster: Lessons from the Edge of Technology* (New York: HarperBusiness, 2001).

43. I also discussed, for example, the following: James Gleick, *Faster: The Acceleration of Just About Everything* (New York: Vintage Books, 1999); and Edward Tenner, *Why Things Bite Back: Technology and the Revenge of Unintended Consequences* (New York: Alfred A. Knopf, 1996); and Diane Vaughan, *The Challenger Launch Decision: Risky Technology, Culture, and Deviance at NASA* (Chicago: University of Chicago Press, 1996).

44. For this discussion, I relied on Daniel Dayan and Elihu Katz, *Media Events: The Live Broadcasting of History* (Cambridge, Mass.: Harvard University Press, 1992).

45. I used the text at www.nara.gov/exhall/charters/declaration/declaration.html.

46. Anthony Lewis, "Taking Our Liberties," *New York Times*, March 9, 2002, A27.

47. Athan G. Theoharis, ed., *A Culture of Secrecy: The Government Versus the People's Right to Know* (Lawrence: University Press of Kansas, 1998).

48. Simson Garfinkel, "How Not to Fight Terror," *Technology Review* 104 (December 2001): 21.

49. William J. Mitchell, *City of Bits: Space, Place, and the Infobahn* (Cambridge, Mass.: MIT Press, 1995) and *e-topia: "Urban Life, Jim—but Not As We Know It"* (Cambridge, Mass.: MIT Press, 2000). The first Mitchell book is out of print, but there is an electronic version at mitpress2.mit.edu/e-books/City_of_Bits/.

Teaching 123

50. Kirk Savage, *Standing Soldiers, Kneeling Slaves: Race, War, and Monument in Nineteenth-Century America* (Princeton, N.J.: Princeton University Press, 1997), 210.

51. I also relied heavily on Kenneth E. Foote, *Shadowed Ground: America's Landscapes of Violence and Tragedy* (Austin: University of Texas Press, 1997).

52. For example, the following appeared too late to use: Allison Gilbert, Phil Hirschkorn, Melinda Murphy, Robyn Walensky, and Mitchell Stephens, eds., *Covering Castrophe: Broadcast Journalists Report September 11* (Chicago: Bonus Books, 2002); Katrina Vanden Heuvel, ed., *A Just Response: The Nation on Terrorism, Democracy, and September 11, 2001* (New York: Thunder's Mouth Press/Nation Books, 2002); *Inside 9-11: What Really Happened by the Reporters, Writers, and Editors of Der Spiegel Magazine* (New York: St. Martin's Press, 2002); and John Prados, ed., *America Confronts Terrorism: Understanding the Danger and How to Think about It; A Documentary Record* (Chicago: Ivan R. Dee, 2002).

53. Edward Yourdon, *Byte Wars: The Impact of September 11 on Information Technology* (Upper Saddle River, N. J.: Prentice Hall, PTR, 2002).

INDEX

ABOUT THE AUTHOR

Richard J. Cox is Professor in Library and Information Science at the University of Pittsburgh, School of Information Sciences, where he is responsible for the archives concentration in the Master's in Library Science degree and the Ph.D. degree. Dr. Cox served as editor of the *American Archivist* from 1991 through 1995, and he is presently editor of the *Records & Information Management Report* as well as serving as the Society of American Archivists Publications Editor. He has written extensively on archival and records management topics and has published eight books in this area: *American Archival Analysis: The Recent Development of the Archival Profession in the United States* (1990), winner of the Waldo Gifford Leland Award given by the Society of American Archivists; *Managing Institutional Archives: Foundational Principles and Practices* (1992); *The First Generation of Electronic Records Archivists in the United States: A Study in Professionalization* (1994); *Documenting Localities* (1996); *Closing an Era: Historical Perspectives on Modern Archives and Records Management* (2000); *Managing Records as Evidence and Information* (2001), winner of the Waldo Gifford Leland Award in 2002; coeditor, *Archives & the Public Good: Records and Accountability in Modern Society* (2002); and *Vandals in the Stacks? A Response to Nicholson Baker's Assault on Libraries* (2002). He is currently working on additional books on the concept of information documents, the impact of electrostatic copying on the modern office, and principled records management (ethical and legal issues).